5-15-94

Sylvia,

You are such a special friend. Thank you for showing me what courage is. 😊

Love,
Debi

Poems
FOR THE
HEALING JOURNEY

by
LANA L. BATEMAN

Edited by
ELLEN W. CAUGHEY

A Barbour Book

© 1992 by Lana L. Bateman

ISBN   1-55748-288-8

Published by Barbour and Company, Inc.
P.O. Box 719
Uhrichsville, Ohio 44683

Cover illustration / design by Drew Winebrenner

Typesetting by Typetronix, Inc., Cape Coral, Florida

Printed in the United States of America

To all who are taking the healing journey, to those who bravely search for lost feelings, and to those with poems yet to be written — we dedicate this book.

CONTENTS

INTRODUCTION

Our Lord is calling us to truth in the innermost being. One pastor used to say, "Some of us are so heavenly minded that we're no earthly good!" While that is a strong statement, many Christians have chosen a spiritual path that excludes emotional growth and change. Unfortunately, self, family, church, and community suffer when that decision is made. Many are emotional wastelands of unresolved pain. While we may appear successful in the workplace, a closer look at our families may show that we lack the ability to feel and communicate with emotional wholeness in healthy relationships.

Those already in the recovery process know that emotional wholeness doesn't happen overnight. If one is willing to embark on the healing journey, working through the pain is essential and requires that we be willing to confront the truth of our situations, however difficult that truth is to face.

In the Bible, Job was an excellent example of such emotional frankness. He often spoke to God of his anger and frustration during the agony of his circumstances. God knows what is buried in our hearts. He wants us to face it, be honest about it, express it in healthy ways, and heal again.

Poems for the Healing Journey was conceived as such an outlet for honest expression. The poems are arranged according to the five stages of a healing journey described in *Bible Promises for the Healing Journey* (Barbour, 1991). When the books are used in tandem, the comfort and reality of God's promises only become more amplified.

Be aware that the truth and reality of soul growth, displayed in the poems of these fellow travelers, is often expressed not in flowery poetic language but through the transparency of free verse. Those who have contributed to this work are courageous Christians who dare to believe the Lord of Gethsemane hears the honest pleas of a wounded heart. At the same time, He is leading each one through dark valleys into the pastures He has promised. (*Note*: Where "General contributor" is given as the poet's name, that person has requested anonymity.)

Don't hesitate to contact a pastor, counselor, close friend, or family member if any of the poems cause pain during your own healing journey. There is wisdom in many counselors and sometimes just sharing at the level of this poetry can move your own heart and surface memories you did not know existed.

May God touch and comfort you on your journey through these words of fellow travelers. Know that you are not alone!

one
PREPARATION

Preparation can be one of the most critical parts of any trip. The journey from past woundedness to wholeness begins with God's call in our hearts.

Just a few years ago, I experienced a growing disquiet that I couldn't understand. To hear that still small voice I needed so much required time alone.

I remember sitting on the bank of a rushing river in Colorado when God placed an undeniable call for more healing in my own life. His message to my heart covers all the areas of preparation listed in this chapter and sets the scene for the poetry to follow. God's challenge to me can be one to all who seek to understand the path of restoration.

God chose nature and poetic language to explain the preparation and cost required for this new step of faith. He used the ways of the forest and the river to illustrate resolve, courage, and commitment. Tenderly affirming His call to heal again, He taught me perseverance and endurance through the example of that funny looking fellow, the beaver.

As I sat at river's edge, listening to classical music and surveying the majesty of God's creation, the following prayer filled my heart.

Lord,

I seem to have spent most of my time at the edge of a rushing river. The sounds of crashing rapids and Vivaldi's trumpets playing in my ear have made me wonder if they were written for each other.

But, today You have brought me to a pastoral place. In contrast to yesterday's powerful rapids, I faintly hear the water flowing in the distance to my right. Barely distinguishable are the sounds of the moving river to my left, while here the waters are almost still. You lead me beside still waters.

I see several beaver dams close by, Lord. What magnificent homes they construct! Behind me there are stumps of trees with teeth marks etched into a point. I can almost see the indomitable creature, gnawing away with his oversized front teeth.

I know he has to build his home, but need the process leave such devastation? The beaver's dam represents the home of your Spirit doesn't it, Lord Jesus? Something has to be destroyed to create it, and sometimes that which has to be felled appears, to human eyes, to be a beautiful thing.

Suddenly You reach into the deep places of my heart.

"The rest of the trees you see are more beautiful because some have been removed. Out of this destruction you think so needless, the beaver's magnificent home is built and the remains show the thinning of My forest. The living trees are now more beautiful because others have been removed.

"So it is with you, my child. There are things within you that may appear to be good but need to be removed so that what remains can be beautiful and useful to me. What the human eye perceives as good is often a distortion, but by My Spirit and your yieldedness, these distortions are exposed and removed. Fear not the process. Like the beaver, keep your eyes and heart on the home and the beauty that surrounds it.

"This little creature's abode is a fortress of power for it can change the flow of a river by divine decree. This particular home is not comely, that looking upon it, you should desire it. But, oh, the wisdom that is hidden there. Safe and secure my little one lives, firmly planted in the midst of a raging river. He is unmoved by the dangers that surround, unconcerned about possible floods, unafraid of what could become of his children or his home should the waters swell and threaten his place of security.

"How differently he would build his home were it built upon fear. Would he build upon the main stream or upon the fast flowing river with its power and majesty? Would he build near the raging rapids? I think not!

"Why do you suppose I planted this little one here? This furry character, insignificant among the giants of my wilderness, is a living testimony to My care. He is a picture of you, My little one.

"The place I have called you to live is not comely that many should desire it. There will be repair and destruction of self to create this home, but all that is left shall burst forth with a beauty that only the touch of My glory can explain.

"Your new home is in a rather precarious place. A mighty river comes against it and flows around it, and yet the river itself must turn in the face of it, shifting the waters that would normally destroy.

"Fear not a coming flood or sudden chaos should giant trees fall near your resting place. None is more secure, even in the face of disaster, than those who live in the hollow of My hand, even in dangerous places.

"Greet every day with My peace as you survey the divine adventure in which I have placed you. Fear not, for I have caused threatening rivers to move aside that your abode should stand. And the floods you fear, these too are in My hands.

"Fear not. For tomorrow is yours and Mine. Rest secure today. And, if tomorrow brings a dangerous swell, then by My power you shall prevail. Through depths of love and visions of My face, the danger will pass.

"Some, terrified, will build their homes in rocky caves. No light or living water dances there. The darkness swallows up one's joy of life and yet the heart shouts, 'Here I am secure!'

"Perhaps you think My tender call will stop if you have chosen caves instead of streams. How little you know the God of grace and love, for you will hear Me reaching out for you among the rocks and cliffs you thought secure.

"My wooing song will echo tenderly, through breezes in the trees and morning stars. The darkness of the cave cannot defeat the distant call of rivers rushing by. Fear not! My songs are not for deafened hearts, but frightened children, fearful of My love and what it asks.

"The river calls. Fear not, for one day very soon you'll meet Me there. And at the river's edge we will rejoice, for it is in this strange precarious place the mystery of My peace will build your home. Here light and water play outside your walls, and rivers step aside at My command. The raging floods cannot destroy you here. Though natural eye might see it as unwise, I prepare this home for you.

One day when darkness seems to overcome, you will respond to all My longing calls and you will deem the river safer still than the solid rock you call security. The river calls, beloved child of Mine. Fear not, for very soon you'll meet Me there."

Those who have responded to the call to face their fears in the healing journey have chosen to meet God at the river's edge. May He now bless you with an understanding of the steps they are taking and with a willingness to hear, should that same appeal for growth begin to summon your own heart.

Cost

Journey

Traveling through life brings many turns.
The smoothness of the road sometimes
     falsely giving comfort.
Suddenly careening curves reminding all
     too quickly that attention is
     needed.
But for those who hunger to celebrate
     God's gift of life; the journey
     impresses one, even though
     weariness seems overwhelming.
We must decide for ourselves.
Do we hunger to be weary from life's
     adventures or do we allow the
     road's turns to leave us weary
     but without hope?

Nancy B. Quinn

A Private Library

Outside
streaked from past thunderstorms.
Inside
smudged with playful fingerprints.
As I enter, I feel the sun's warm rays
stream through the glass panes of an unfamiliar room.
Stacked high are the periodicals, newspapers and clippings . . .
most important happenings in some sort of order yet undetectable.
Very strange, almost eerie place,

attic air and dust spectacles dance through the paths of light
and settle carelessly onto the oak planked floor.

Undisturbed, long since deserted, shying,
yet almost anxiously awaiting courage to unlock the silence
and release the secrets of this carefully preserved reality.
Many other rooms, chambers and nooks, filled to overflowing
invite cautious entry through slivered yonder doors.
Books, books, and more books stand at attention, ever attuned
for the anticipated command to at last reveal their inner truths.
Forever suspended, long snapshot covered hallways
and creaky spiral stairwells search for the master room with index
unfolding in patterned fashion a private library.

Is it true?

Has the heart of the matter been strengthened
enough to sustain the overwhelming emotion needed for the
discovery
of the lost, hidden, the shamed and the cherished secrets
of the private library of my soul?

Yes, for on the mantle the gears grind,
the clock starts ticking,
the work has already begun.
Your grace was sufficient after all . . . .

Kay Kocour

Will I Still See You?

Lord, You say I'm wounded deep within . . .
> that I must humble my heart
>> and let someone come alongside.

I'm frightened of the dreams . . .
> that have already begun to fill my nights.

If I let You open the bars of bronze
> so carefully defending those long buried memories . . .

Will I die . . .
> or want to??

Will I still see You
> if the terror seems to overwhelm me . . .
>> and the pain becomes consuming?

To have to wonder what is there . . .
> spins me out of control.

Can I bear to speak the words of my darkness to another?
> Can I bear to hear them myself . . .??

With only a tiny mustard seed of faith . . .
> I whisper, "I'll try."

It is because You go with me . . . that I can dare to go.
> The journey into unknown thoughts is only possible . . . . .
>> because You know me . . . . You love me.

I know that I must face . . .
> and feel . . . the pain.

Please don't let me run from what you faced so willingly . . .
> on Calvary.

Help me be still . .
> as You heal my heart once again
>> in deeper . . .
>>> and deeper places.

And when the tear-filled days of pain have passed,
> and raging rivers finally grow calm
restore me once again to gentle peace
> and all that I have known of Your sweet love.

General contributor

The Room

I've opened the door to a room closed so long.
My weak heart is racing. There's sweat on my palm.
So many voices have warned, "Don't go in!"
But one still, small voice says it's time to begin.
The light from the hallway shows outlines and shades
Of piles everywhere tumbling down in cascades.
The clutter is scattered from ceiling to floor
From corner to corner clear up to the door.
The sight of it all shoots through me with pain.
A life was shut down here. I see the blood stain.
An endless endeavor to bury and hide
Haunting reminders they failed when they tried.
There in the midst of the mess opened wide
Is a book on relationships stained where they've cried.
The room must be cleaned. I know in my heart.
But I'm overwhelmed. I can't even start.
The job is too big. The assignment's too tough.
I didn't dream it would be quite this rough.
Just as I'm quietly closing the door
That soft, subtle voice speaks to me once more.
"Child, though this room is beyond man's repair
You'll delight when you yield it to God's loving care."
Gently and slowly He leads me right in
And we stand in the midst of the hurt and the sin.
I hold tight to His hand, feeling weak in my knees.
He gathers me into His arms. I'm so pleased.
But He carries me straight to the place that's blood red
And He says, "This is my blood. It was here it was shed."

[continued]

This is the place where you must begin.
There's no other place where one enters in.
Weeping I cry, "Why not my clean room?"
Whispering He says, "New life springs from a tomb."
His hand on my shoulders, He contacts my eyes,
"The children who watch Me are the ones who are wise.
All you must do is listen to Me.
The room will take care of itself. You will see.
The key to its cleaning is not in your hand,
But in following the Master at healing the land."
With trembling and fear I gaze into His eyes
And I enter the tomb knowing well I will rise.

Linda O'Toole

"Here is a trustworthy saying: If we died with him, we
will also live with him." *2 Timothy 2:11* (NIV)

Resolve

Make My Life A Butterfly

Make my life a Butterfly
Oh Lord of my mind

From thoughts of despair
    to the hope of the cross
From worried confusion
    to confident trust

Make my life a Butterfly
Oh Lord of my body

From sickness and sorrow
    to health and vigor
From feeble muscles
    to capable strength

Make my life a Butterfly
Oh Lord of my soul

From apathetic indifference
    to action-conviction
From fickle Lordship
    to constant obedience

Make my life a Butterfly
Oh Lord of my work

From lack of direction
    to centered focus
From self-centered ambition
    to selfless service

Make my life a Butterfly
    and I will be
Fit for service
    unto Thee.

Christine D'Amico

Winner

(Philippians 4:13)

Behind a winner is a winner.

What is a winner?

One who is able to rise above the circumstances
life presents.

One who is able to grow and mature in spirit,
mind and body into a specific understanding
midst the storms and after the storms are spent.

Focused.
Determined.
Resolved.

Is it free?

Can you find this ability in a jar or mail-order this quality — COD?

Or, is it developed,
as a photograph in and out of various solutions
and hung to dry with skilled hands at last evolves in
darkness into its finished form.

Of this ability I know one thing,

it develops not alone
for behind every winner
there is a winner.

Kay Kocour

I Fix My Eyes On Him

(Hebrews 12:11–13)

My spiritual walk has a slight limp.
For many years the damage went untreated, and
I was forced to live with the pain that
Tore my spirit and damaged my emotions.
Looking casually, you might not see it.
Only if you dare walk with me will you see
The truth, for I have become adept at
Covering up my handicaps behind walls and masks.
When I try to go too fast, or attempt to
Take long strides past what I can handle . . .
The hidden becomes obvious.
Reminded often of my weaknesses, the only
Solution and comfort I have must be to
Depend on God for support and relief.
He calls out, in love, for me to slow down
Instead of awkwardly running in this anguished gait.
And He bids me to take His hand when my
Endurance is gone and I've stopped progressing.
He alone knows what I can endure and
Whispers that I must trust Him if I
Am to continue to press on.
Traveling with the giants of scripture, I see
How God's grace and power transform . . .
To glorify and demonstrate His perfect purpose.
As I move along life's sometimes hard and
Threatening path . . . my prayer is this:
That I may always lean on my Lord.
For as I yield myself to Him, I envision
That glorious day when He will make me whole
As He carries me Home.
—Until that time I need never walk alone.
My Lord Jesus is my doctor, coach, and friend.
As I fix my eyes on Him . . .
In my heart I FLY!!!

Jo Winkowitsch

As I Walk By Faith

The flood and the fire assail me
Though I cry out, I do not despair.
For even in harsh, raging waters, God will
Keep me from drowning.
Although in the midst of intense flames,
I will not be overcome.
For I can walk on water if I
Heed my Master's call to come to Him.
And I can bear to travel in the roaring
Fire, if my Lord walks along with me.
I will not be swept away . . .
For He has not given us a spirit of fear.
I will not be left alone . . .
For He has promised He will not forsake us.
He is always there . . . leading . . . caring . . .
Encouraging . . . comforting . . . uplifting . . .
I am safe with Him, no matter what
The circumstance or condition.
For truly He will make a way out of any
And all distress as I look to Him.
I must remember that, as the waters rise,
. . . As the fire blazes on,
God's plans for us are good.
NOTHING takes Him by surprise.
Together with Him, I can face anything
For He has offered to bring me through.
As I go on with a hope and a future,
He will remain near, to strengthen, and to teach
What I must know to live the abundant
Christian life, as I walk by faith with Him.

Isaiah 43:2   Zechariah 10:11   Jeremiah 29:11

Jo Winkowitsch

God Does Not Burn Out

I have determined that I must live life
To the fullest, as I let God fill my
Mind with thoughts of Him.
I envision and welcome His rich mercy,
Forgiveness and love . . . poured out
FOR me, INTO me, and THROUGH me,
As I am emptied of myself.
I will strive to be all God wants
Without wishing the fight was over.
I do not want to waste these precious
Days and memories by ungratefulness.
Let me learn this lesson well, dear God,
I DO want to live . . .
I have just been scared by road blocks,
With You by my side I can go past them,
As I press on to follow You . . . .
For You know the way I should go.
I will not be afraid.
I will not run away.
I will not give up on You.
I must just keep my eyes on You as we
Grow ever nearer my final destination.
And until then, my heart will go on singing,
As I walk in faith (hand in hand,
Shoulder to shoulder), in the family and
Army of the Lord who called us out of darkness.
And in doing so, I will lose my own life
To gain Your most abundant life . . .
Motivate me for service by Your God-breathed love
Which remains my source . . . to shine forth
Freely, as I live my life for You in this
Light-rejecting world.
Help me remember that Your light will not go out!
For You do not forsake Your children,
As You pass through the sea of distress and
Affliction at the head of Your people.
Let me always dwell on Your love and
Keep my eyes on You . . . 1 Peter 2:9-10

Jo Winkowitsch

Unexpected Friends

Hurt became my friend today
Grasped my neck and hugged me tight
Before —
I'd push and run from her and hide
I hated her ugly sight.
Fearful of when she'd pop up again
I'd do
        say
        and be all the right things,
        I thought.
Yet, hurt found me out
And I stopped — exhausted
Collapsing under her weight.
A weight too heavy to outrun.
So I grasp her.
And won't let her leave
Until every tear has been stilled.

Lois C. Muhasky

Courage

Victory

The battle has begun, Lord
I have not asked for it —
                    nor wanted it.

My shield is tarnished,
My sword is dull.

Lord, clothe me with Your armor.
How perfectly it fits and
                    protects me.

With Your strength I will stand,
With Your courage I will fight.

The battle may be won or lost
But the Victory is ours!

Linda Mae Richardson
(Cancer patient)

Bird Songs

In the deep of the night

a Nightingale lifts a song to you

In the dark a lonesome lark

strains to find his key.

Psalms are readily sung

at the breaking of dawn's light

but it takes a brave little bird

to sing while it's still night.

Kay Kocour

Because You Have Hope

The Lord's will be done.
Not mine, or the way I want things to be.
But the Lord's.
That's a tough pill to swallow sometimes,
For I would have every day a happy one
With no call for tears or heartache.
I would not ever want to
See you suffering.
Yet, I see the Lord's purposes are different.
I look only to my selfish desires and
The Lord's plan takes in all eternity.
For if He allows us to suffer
We also know that He will help us and
Give us the strength to go on.
Never doubting Him. . . always trusting Him.
So don't be afraid of the future.
Keep your heart and mind fixed on Jesus.
He will guide you, He will uphold you
While He takes your burdens from you.
And if things don't work out the way
You would have them . . .
Remember that the pain and grief we
Endure during this short stay on earth
Is nothing compared to the glory
Awaiting us in heaven.
I pray that you will have courage
Because the Lord is watching over you.
. . . And peace, because you have hope.
The hope that is in our Lord, who will not
Let us suffer without a purpose.
And through the strength of God,
I pray that you might be able to say,
As I have,
The Lord's will be done.

Jo Winkowitsch

Commitment

I Will

I will praise you
I will trust you
Whether feelings come or go
I will walk the paths before me
For I'm in Your hands . . . . . I know.

Rita McIlwain

Commitment

A commitment to anything is an unwavering application
of mind, body, and soul with sufficient supplication.
A double-minded soul does not succeed in any task
with his time lock securely anchored in the future or the past.
So if you wish success to follow in your chosen fields,
submit your will to the One who to His Father did yield.
And with your heart commit to The Kingdom, renew your troubled mind,
and the success you will experience will surely pass the test of time.

Kay Kocour

From This Day

I promise to be supportive

yet give you room to grow,

to nurture and protect

the commitment seeds we'll sow.

And I'll cherish our time together

as golden moments from above,

moments from the storehouse

of our Father's love.

My trust I place with you Lord

to accomplish that which today begins,

And I'll thank you always for your sufficient grace

and for the chance to start again.

Kay Kocour

Song Of Ruth

I love you, Lord.

    I Praise Your Holy Name.

I thank you, Lord,

    for choosing me

        and for calling me on!

There is no turning back.

Refiner's Fire ROAR!

    Consume all the dross from my life.

    Take those childhood vows that

        I made for survival.

I desire to be totally yours.

Your face is all I seek!

Ruth McMath

The Witness

"Try Jesus," Grandma said,
"But be sure to cut your fingernails,
and wear long sleeves,
and go to him
with your face pale and serious."

"Try Jesus," the bumper sticker said,
on the car
that passed me going 70 miles an hour,
nearly running me off the road.

"Try Jesus," the blond,
well-bred church worker said,
as she gave me a crisp, hurting criticism,
and smiled condescendingly.

"Try Jesus," the teen group said,
as they passed me hurriedly
and ignored the lonely newcomer
who watched them longingly.

"Try Jesus," my Christian fellow-workers said,
as they hurried to their classes
on self-improvement,
while I ate and worked alone.

"Try Jesus," said a loving friend,
who stood by me when no one else did.
"Try Jesus," she said softly, "He loves you
just as you are."

Which one could I believe?

Betty Reber

The Sun just rising in the East,
Is sinking in the West.
The clock announcing Dawn's first light,
Is chiming Evening's Feast.
My feet, all Pink in baby shoes,
Are gnarled and tired and worn.
The Path of Life now seems so short
That once appeared so long!
And soon — perhaps just round the Bend
Or up the "Climbing Hill";
I'll hear His Voice speak forth the Words;
PEACE, MY CHILD . . . BE STILL!
So, rise my Soul and dance my Heart;
Praise Him while you may!
The Night's Far Spent and soon will dawn
THE EVERLASTING DAY!
Let not one Hour seed forth and flower,
Nor pass as Dust away —
THAT DOES NOT SAY, "I LOVE YOU LORD!
I WILL THY WILL AND WAY!"

Dorothy M. Owen

Support

Sharing

Understanding eyes that see beyond the image.

Patient ears that hear silent tears from the soul.

Soft words that send encouragement and gentle guidance.

Loving arms that embrace and hold secure.

A warm heart that bleeds sincerity.

Strong feet willing to walk an extra mile.

Where will the journey take you, my friend?

Soar high above the mountain tops and know you are truly living life.

Jeanne Linnemanstons

How Like A Gardenia

White petals,

nestle gently midst the cool deep green.

Richly pure,

the contrast takes my breath

and your sweet fragrance lingers

long after my thoughts turn to practical matters.

Kay Kocour

On This Day

Mend a quarrel.

Search out a forgotten friend.

Dismiss a suspicion and replace it with trust.

Write a letter to someone who misses you.

Encourage a youth who has lost faith.

Keep a promise.

Forget an old grudge.

Examine your demands on others and vow to reduce them.

Fight for a principle.

Express your gratitude.

Overcome an old fear.

Take two minutes to appreciate the beauty of nature.

Tell someone you love them.

Tell them again,

And again,

And again.

Frank R. Zelarney

The Keys

If I had the keys to heaven,
I'd open its treasure store
and shower you with stardust,
moonbeams and much much more.
I'd crush the petals of the mountain flower
store its fragrance just for you
I'd capture the cool of the evening
and refresh you with morning dew.

Now I'm not one to worship a tool
used in The Carpenter's hand
but to honor a vessel of obedience
seems right, this much I can . . .
a tool . . . a chisel, a hammer, THE FIRE!
Can't deny the Almighty's power!!
Yielding to the molder's molding
is what His heart desires.

And even though the miles are between us
I still feel your warmth and care.
Even when I try to deny it . . .
a supply is always there
to comfort the pain, release the shame
quiet the bell of hell.

Know my friend . . . I know you're not my savior
but my savior within you . . . dwells.

Kay Kocour

In God We Trust

I would have despaired
    had I not seen the goodness
        of my God in the land of the living.

I would have despaired
    had You not taken my hand
        to steady my heart when all seemed lost.

I would have despaired
    if You had left me to my fractured thoughts
    with no hope of finding that place of peace
        where Your heart meets mine
           down deep inside.

I would have despaired
    if you hadn't promised me safety
        beneath Your massive wings
           when storms assailed my soul
            and
                life secure became a faded dream.

If I couldn't have somehow trusted You . . .
    I would have despaired.

Lana Bateman

Pecking Through The Shell

"She's almost here," the people cry
as they stand around my egg, the egg
that still encompasses me,
sometimes I hear them beg,

"Please help her, God, set her free
have mercy on your child,"
and my pecking efforts multiply,
Tap! Tap! my beak goes wild.

Tap! Tap! Poke! Poke! I bang my head,
the only part that moves,
my wings are plastered to my sides,
some days my strength improves

so much that cramped inside the egg
I push with every limb,
more cracks appear, freedom looks near,
then I tire and my hopes turn dim.

"She'll never make it — is it worth it?"
they whisper, but I hear,
Worse yet, they tire and leave me, calling
"We'll come back later, dear."

How can I blame them? I too lose hope.
How long this process, rebirth?
The egg runs blood, it stinks of sulfur.
Is freedom really worth

all this pain — this agony,
this waiting without end,
that tortures not only the fetus
but family and friend?

"Oh, please don't leave," I cry out
from inside my prison shell.
"You're my pom-pom girls, my cheerleaders
and my Lamaze partners as well."

They laugh at this new humor,
(Oh, some of them go away)
but the others work out schedules
so that one will always stay

beside the egg that holds me.
Sometimes, peering through a crack
I see someone's eyes look into my own
and someone whispers,

"Welcome back!"

Janice Gail Knowlton

A Friend

A friend is special
  and very rare —
when in need,
    they're always there.

A friend listens
    within their heart
no matter the distance —
    you're never apart.

A special touch
    allows the tears,
holds the hand
    and calms the fears.

Encourages adventure
    to try something new
a friend is interested
    in being with you.

Laughs at the jokes,
    feels the pain;
a truly good friend . . .
    will always remain.

Eve Bailey

Perseverance

Darkness Has No Handles

Compose in prose

Deep deep darkness, drifting soul.

Eyelids close

Inky blackness, false repose.

Nocturnal Rider

Press on . . . . press on,

Hurry friend, bring forth the dawn.

Kay Kocour

Through The Window Of My Soul

Writing and writing

Twelve hours at a time —

Some in prose, and

Some in rhyme.

Many memories

Go back in time —

Some are more recent,

But all are mine.

I'm working through feelings

And trying to heal —

Coming out of my numbness,

And starting to feel.

It's a scary time,

And so revealing —

I hope and pray

It will hasten my healing.

gloria f. parker

Paralyzed

Paralysis.
It's like this.
It's a kiss
of the serpent,
a snake
whose fangs
release
a
numbing
toxin.

It numbs
the body,
sometimes
the mind.
For a time

we can't move.
Want to,
but can't.
We can't feel,
want to
but can't.

And having
paralyzed us
the snake
has its way
with us.

HAD
its way
with us.

But this,
this
paralysis
is
different.

The paralysis
of healing.
God saying,
Lie still
my child.
Rest.
Be still
I will let you know
when to rise.

You
and only
you
will know
when you're healed.

(A poem for my friends who don't understand why "will power" can't force us to go on once we are in recovery and memories/traumas emerge for resolution. Why we're not "lazy" or "stubborn." We're Paralyzed.)

Janice Gail Knowlton

The Fighter's Treasure

When at the end of my life I pause,
And consider what's gone by,
I will think of and yearn for the time
When the fight in me ran high.

Yes in spite of this life's pain,
And the tiresome days come and gone,
I'll yearn to battle once again,
And to sing that fighter's song.
For the victory with all of its comforts,
And the rest that there I'll find
Cannot be compared with the battle,
That is fought with my Savior in mind.

A peaceful prayer made in calmness,

In the peace of a quiet place,

Is not quite as close as a desperate plea,

When my foe I do meet face to face.

So give me the battle with all its terror,

Yes give me the fight for its tears,

For all those times of fight and struggle,

Are the treasures of my years.

Andrew H. Stone

Endurance

Come O Life

I am thankful for the trials that have come into my life
I must not refuse them entrance
For it is in their presence that I am purged, purified and
      pruned
It is in their midst that I see the power and know the
      sufficiency of My God.

I will walk whatever paths are set before me
For to stay in my place — free from hurdles
is to live a shallow existence
Never entering into the depths of life and purpose that are
      meant to be ours in Christ Jesus.

So Come O Life . . . I welcome you
For I walk your paths not alone
But with the hand of My God
Holding me tight.

Rita McIlwain

Touch Me Not

"Touch me not," said Jesus
as Mary put out her hand.
Her touch would have propelled her
into another land

another place of being
beyond the earthly vale.
Jesus knew that Mary
must continue in travail.

As a living, breathing woman
alive in every way
she could share the Savior's message
with the people who would stay

here on this earth to lead us
in the paths of righteousness.
"Touch me not," said Jesus
to the woman He would bless

with the message of salvation
through His resurrected form.

"Touch me not."

yet through the centuries

His touch would keep us warm.

Janice Gail Knowlton

Where Are You?

My soul refuses to be comforted;
There is no one to call me forth from my grave;
Death and despair are all about me;
I am oppressed by their heaviness!

My cry is, "My God, my God, why have you forsaken me?"
    "How long must I have this unbearable pain?"

Yet I will trust in you
       for I am convinced that you will again return me
           to the land of the living.

Ruth McMath

Out Of The Abyss

Anguish of depression enslaved me.

Others have had to walk there.

Much later happiness has come

And we are more fully aware —

Of the beauty that surrounds us

On faces of loved ones and friends

And in wondrous sights of nature

Where colors perfectly blend.

Without walks through the valleys

Mountains would never be climbed

Peace, understanding, and purpose

Would elude till the end of time.

There'd be no basking in glory

While panoramas parade in view

And no multitude of blessings

For strength to carry us through.

Laura V. Jansen

two
PROVISIONS

We have a faithful God Who gives and draws forth from us that which will be needed for healing in our lives. Often, as you will see in the poetry that follows, He has already placed the needed provisions inside us. At the proper time, as each becomes appropriate for restoration, He calls them forth.

Scripture tells us in Romans 8:24c-25 that true hope is trusting God for what we do not yet see or have not experienced. The poems that address *hope*, the first provision, speak of the times in recovery when one is able to sense, perhaps in the smallest way, that light will shine again. It is not too late to heal again, grow again, be useful again, or have that treasured second chance.

Hebrews 11:1 tells us that *faith* is being sure of what we hope for and certain of what we cannot see. These poems express the certainty that God is with us as we heal and sees our faith, no matter how small. We find that no darkness can ultimately keep Him from delivering us, and we can see through the eyes of a child that our faith can have many colors.

As we move on to *honesty*, these poems reveal the writers' struggles to face reality and themselves honestly before God. Some describe a need finally to be able to cry or feel, while others long for the courage to speak out even in times of weakness. All share a need to be accepted and to experience true and healthy love in spite of past dysfunction.

Safety is a significant concern to all in the healing process. Those moving toward wholeness share their safety in Jesus, a safety that endures through the storms of pain and reconstruction. This safety is so real and warm that, in times of great questioning, even to the edge of despair, Jesus still gives us the freedom and permission to feel the emotions and to express what is in our hearts.

The poems of *relief* show dawning rays that indicate we will live again. The difficulties of past abuse cannot keep the sun from shining forever. Our God indeed is the ultimate answer and He longs for us to approach Him as Abba (Daddy). He gently calls us to have the heart of a child and to find a child's needed rest and relief in Him.

Openness is being willing to see the effects of our own shallowness and yet long for a spiritual and emotional depth that is God-breathed. Openness can also allow God to bring to our awareness whatever may be buried inside, such as pain, tears, anger, and even feelings of futility or failure.

We long for the *comfort* our Lord can give as we face the abuse in our lives. There are many arenas of loss, shame, grief, or terror that only He can comfort. The prose and poetry of this section share the ways in which God has personally comforted those who long to understand how such hurt, or violence, could be perpetrated against a child or an adult. Comfort also includes the ways our Lord provides cherished friends, basic necessities, or material gifts in the midst of our sorrow and distress. His message begins to break through the walls of pain . . . we will live again!

The last section of this chapter is one long ago discarded by many Christians, *permission to feel*. Sometimes we condemn ourselves, thinking a real believer in Jesus Christ should be capable of only good feelings and incapable of any emotions or feelings that appear negative. Sadly, it is not until we are honest with God about our true feelings that we can accept our humanity. With that acceptance comes the realization that churches are not filled with saints but with sinners saved by grace. And the grace that saved us came from One Who cried, "My God, My God, why has Thou forsaken me?" (*Matthew 27:46*) In that one question, our Lord not only gave us permission to feel but also to ask, "Why?"

What a God we have! Yes, the ultimate victory is His, but the journey to that victory is ours. Trust the provisions He is adding to or calling forth from you as the process continues.

Sometimes He will lead by fire, other times by clouds. The road is seldom easy, but ultimately it leads you right to the heart of Jesus, the greatest provision of all.

Remember: If any of these poems surface unexplainable pain, buried memories of abuse, or other feelings of deep loss, please contact a counselor, pastor, or friend to come alongside. It could be a very important step in your own healing journey.

Hope

A Fragile Hope

Safe place. . .
              safe place . . .
                          safe place. . . .

A curly headed cherub
              is crying out for rest . . .
                          grown tired of the weight of woman's soul.

Now stretching on the tips of toes
              full-panicked from the strain,
                          too small to bear a burden this intense.

How can she stay up on her toes that long. . .
                          with body now so large
                          and hair so gray?

No wonder she's grown weary balanced there,
              for how much can a little one endure . . .
                          of weight so overwhelmingly unfair?

And where have toys of passing childhood gone . . .
              when tiny legs could dance with sheer delight
                          and feet were weary only from one's play?

Can pain erase such joys
              with one broad stroke . . .
                          to leave behind the shock of middle-age . . .
                                      [continued]

of wrinkled hands
            and
                eyes that cannot see?

Or does it turn in time to fragile hope
                for ravaged childlike heart
                    to see through blooming eyes

        that elderly facades need not be graves

                and tiny feet can grow . . .

                        to dance again.

                    Lana Bateman

The Box

It's Christmas again.

Our friendly tree glows each night . . . and underneath its protective boughs sit beautifully wrapped boxes, awaiting anxious fingers. Little ones who tear off coverings with high pitched squeals of delight.

But in the far dark corner, I see another box, visible only to me; such a mysterious contrast to the many gaily adorned neighbors that surround it.

My box has wrapping, too. There seems to be layers tattered, faded, and torn as if many times the attempt had been made to open the box and allow its contents to be revealed, awakened and set free. But, alas, it had only been an effort made. For my box remains covered in its wraps.

I notice one layer of paper decorated with clowns — clowns with sorrowful eyes. I see black paper — so black that it can hide secrets in its darkness. I see colorless paper revealing nothing — only quiet wandering emptiness.

Yes, my box has ribbon, too, ribbons of string, strings that have bound this weary box for oh so long. Sprinkled over the top, there appears to be the dust of glittering diamonds, but to the sensitive soul . . . crystallized tears of pain and sorrow that have not yet melted way.

Oh box what shall I do with you? I want to throw you away never to be tormented by you again, but I smile, because I know that is impossible for I live in you . . . . my weary box.

But wait, under the tree I notice something else. Sitting there so quiet and nonthreatening, humble and tender is the same manger scene I have placed under the tree for so many years. The babe is in the manger; a heavenly glow surrounds His face. Oh, the love that must have filled His tiny heart.

[continued]

There is hope!

Box look!
There is hope . . .

My weary box . . . turns . . . and smiles.

Merry Christmas Box.

Rita McIlwain

Daisies

Silly daisies,
    It's autumn!
Your blooming time
    Is Spring.
Thank you,
    For each smiling face
    Nodding hope.
I too, long to bloom,
    And for me,
    It's autumn.

Betty Reber

The Gospel Settles It All

He does not read your mail

He does not tap your phone

He does not talk to your neighbors

Or peep through your blinds

The Word of God always finds

The heart in need

The troubled mind

He is seeking the willing, the feeble

The unloved, the lame, the poor, the maimed

The Word of God is calling all

When the sermon ended was your life aired

Don't fret, nobody there cared

You see everyone was brought there to

hear the same story

Of defeat, Triumph, and Glory! ! ! ! ! !

Lloyd H. Thomas, Sr.

Another Chance

The Lord is good
A merciful Father
beyond our comprehension.
How He wove into our paths,
yet, another chance
broken vessels
unintentioned
caring, tenderhearted from our youth
but like most
filled with broken parts.
Broken parts can't make good choices
though they try so hard.
He knew. He cared.
In despair on appointed days,
they each asked God why.
His love said,
"Just be Mine,
Don't try.
Let me heal you, love you, fill you
Then let me bless you
With yet, another chance."

Diane Thompson

New Life

The rose will bloom again
   Although
Trampled down, uprooted, disregarded
  once a thing of beauty —
   Now
Bruised, battered, and broken —
   Replanted
Leaning into the sun, feeling warmth,
  Soft rain, and loving care.

Tender leaves begin to glisten —
  Buds show promise of beauty restored.
   Petals with exquisite texture,
    And the color of scarlet.
Fragrant, radiant, highly esteemed —
   Again
Faith has won the Victory —
   New life
Manifested in a perfected Rose.

Frances Moss Taylor

Faith

Rebirth

In the depths of the pit — life stirs
As a soul cries to the Lord.
Born with tears
Shed of fear
And cleansed by the Saviour's Blood.

In the depths of the soul
A new garden grows
Planted by God's hand and fed by the Water of Life.

For you see —
there is no pit too deep for Jesus to reach
No sin so black that when confessed with repentant heart —
that God cannot forgive
And clothed with Christ's very robe of righteousness
We begin anew — a new child of creation.

Jan Barnes

Reward

"You get what you pay for . . . ."
a friend once said, "you'll see."
But I was purchased by the blood
that was shed on a tree at Calvary.
What would He want with me?
How could I ever be?
justified to be in His sight?
How could I ever stand the light
Of His righteousness, majesty,
omnipotence and might?

Well, here we are awaiting our reward
for treasures we've bestowed.
He looks over mine . . . . I can't look . . . .
my eyes remaining closed.
"Look, an iota of intention,
a pence of peace, a cent of sense,
and even more, let's see . . . .
spangles of sorrow, rosettes of remorse
and pecks of prayer," He says.
"are pleasing to me."

"But over here my child
is what justifies you to be in my sight
making you able to stand the light
of my righteousness, majesty, omnipotence and might."

I open my eyes slowly
not wishing to be too bold . . . .
and behold . . . . a farthing of faith and a tittle of trust
is the only treasure that He holds.

Kay Kocour

On Wings Of Wind

On wings of the wind God did fly
To deliver me;
Upon a Cherub riding high
He set this captive free.

He breathed fire from His nose,
Angry toward my foe,
God stood aloft with mighty pose
And made him let me go!

The earth did shake, hills did fall,
Arrows from His quill
God used all these and thunder squalls;
My foe God's wrath did fill!

I was almost beaten down,
But God allowed it not.
My foe was dashed upon the ground,
And I the victory got!

On wings of wind my God does ride
Watching over me;
Upon a Cherub riding
He gives the victory!

(Based on Psalm 18:1-12, especially v.10)

Kenneth R. Thompson

My Faith Is Plaid

My faith is not one color
My faith is plaid you see,
I like to celebrate all forms
of Christianity.

I love my church that's Catholic,
My church that's on T.V.
My church that's in a public park,
My church that's within me.

There's room in me for lots of God,
But just one God above,
The one who sent me Jesus,
So I'd know His constant love.

Janice Gail Knowlton
(at nine years old)

Times Of Exposure

The pristine pine and stubborn oak
frame a maple's glory.

Solely she is standing
to tell a season's story.

Each leaf as a chapter drifts slowly down
until there are no more.

Stark she stands,
unashamed,
rooted in the promises of spring.

Kay Kocour

Honesty

Erosion

The saddest part is,
    that sometime,
    when I wasn't watching,
She slipped away,
    particle by particle.
Now all I have left
    is a stranger,
And I must care for her,
    while my heart slips away
    particle by particle,
Wishing hopelessly
    that I had her back,
    whole again,
    even for a few moments.
But as with all life,
This is the fullest moment
    I have.
Life's erosion is constant,
    but so subtle,
That we turn
    from a meaningless distraction,
    to look back at it,
    and gasp in horror,
    "Where did it go?"

Betty Reber

Prayer For A Friend

I've a friend, dear Lord, who is facing a war

That You can help her win, I'm sure.

It's bedtime now; but here I kneel

And cannot sleep because I feel

Her need so deeply. She and I

Have been asking, "How?" and "Where?" and "Why?"

Often enough these days, that we

Must have asked all the questions there can be.

We need more faith! for it is You

Who can see the problem and help us through

And make things beautiful that now

Seem anything but that. Yet how

Shall we come to You? And, too,

What shall we say or think or do?

[continued]

You knew these questions long ago.

Before I even think, YOU KNOW.

Before I ever was born, YOU ARE.

You see things clearly from afar.

In Your wonderful greatness You choose to love

My friend and me; and up above,

You see this crisis. So I leave

The problem with You, and believe

That You will make this darkness light

And make us to praise Your name. Good night.

M. I. Martin

Tears Unshed

I have seen the result of unshed tears buried deep
into dishonest souls covered o'er in disbelief
and as they harden through the years midst a moan their seeds are sown
and they produce a bitter fruit . . . . behold, a heart of stone.

Now who could prescribe such a natural relief?
Who subscribes healing to the tears of belief . . . .
cleansing the countenance of brokenness and strife
while softening hearts with future hope . . . . and a satisfying life.

Fellow travelers of peaks and valleys with honesty of feeling do rely,
for before a soul is vested in hope, it first must be able to cry.

Kay Kocour

Straining To Be

Straining to see the child in me
the years have hid her well
the one who all the people know
is not the one to tell
your lies, excuses, and complaints
increase the pain within
but daddy told me to be strong
and you must fight to win.

When effort and a friendly grin
are used to pacify
the anger still remains inside
and this I can't deny
words and gestures meant to say
"I love you, you are great!"
Often follow attempts to cheer
or sometimes to sedate.

How will I know a love that is
so unlike all the rest?
For I want to be a family member
no longer just a guest.

Diana Williams

I am a weak servant, Lord
    I whine
    I cry
    I strike out in anger
    I retaliate
    and pain depresses me.
Can you use this poor weak servant, Lord?
    who desires to serve you?
    who wants to grow in wisdom and knowledge?
    who is eager for a close relationship with you?
I am yours, Lord . . .
Use me to your glory.

Jackie Bush

Safety

He Does Safely Keep

Jesus took me in His arms,
While He took up my fight
When my fears caused great alarm
And brought my heart such fright.

Then He gently lowered me
To His bosom kind;
From my fears He set me free
As I, His rest did find.

There's no place I'd rather be
Than with my Savior sweet,
When in the rolling, raging sea
My life, He safely keeps.

Kenneth R. Thompson

Lord, I Believe

At loose ends and asking questions
That I never thought I would
Do I dare to doubt your promise
To work all things for my good?

Now the truth I built my life on
Seems threadbare and wearing thin —
Peace that passes understanding . . .
Will I know that peace again?

Jesus, let me ask my questions,
Hear my anger, help me grieve
In the freedom your love gives me,
Let me say Lord, I believe.

Like the sun comes up at dawning
Bringing light to darkened eyes
For a moment I can see you . . .
In your Truth I fear no lies.

"Child, I chose you and I called you,
Gave you life — I know your name.
When you seek me, you will find me.
My love for you will never change."

And He let me ask my question,
Heard my anger, helped me grieve
In the freedom His love gave me
I could say Lord I believe.

Lord, you let me ask my questions
Hear my anger, help me grieve
In the freedom you still give me
I will say, "Lord, I believe."

Kathy Dixon Henderson

Relief

The Cat

the cat was endlessly lying in wait
invading obscure corners
seeking narrow openings
pouncing without warning

momentarily darkness lifted
my fears were allayed
perhaps freedom was imminent
    but
        the cat was endlessly lying in wait
        bringing maladies of the body
            disorders of the mind
        terrible diseases of the soul

how could I escape the cat?
where could I hide?
the answer came so simply:
the cat cannot harm you
if you are prepared for him
    now
        the cat is endlessly lying in wait
    but
        I am armed and ready to meet him

forever darkness has lifted
my fears removed
freedom, no longer a dream.

Brenda Picazo

Integrity (is a full course meal)

Complete

served a mousse in crystal dish.

I stretched, pushed back from the dining table

assessing my gains and losses as I sipped my tea.

Contentment

brought the reckoning of the bill of fare.

A generous gratuity was graciously accepted

by all involved.

Satisfied,

I strode to greet the evening

and to my surprise,

the evening greeted me.

Kay Kocour

He's Alive

Morn calls to the dawn
Light streams past proud Caesar's stone
The tomb is empty.

Kay Kocour

Bliss

How delighted I am, to know whose I am
To know where I was and to know
I am not there anymore! ! ! ! ! !

Lloyd H. Thomas, Sr.

Jesus Came

I played in the world and got dirty.

Thinking there was no one to clean me up.

I fell and got hurt.

Thinking no one heard my cries.

I tried to run and hide.

Thinking no one would find me.

Then Jesus came to wash my sins away.

Jesus came to wipe the tears away.

Jesus came to find and show me the way.

Patricia Piedra

Your Daddy Knows

Lord, sometimes I get so weary
With all that life demands;
The house, the car, the kids, the yard
The bills and future plans.

My faith wanes and my fight is gone.
My fears, they all run wild.
That's when I need to hear You say,
"It's time to be a child."

"It's time to climb up in My lap and
Let Me stroke your hair.
Now, snuggle up against My chest.
Feel the safety there?

"Be still while Abba tells you
All about the time
When long before the world began,
I loved you, in My mind.

"I couldn't wait to birth you,
I had planned you for so long
And the day you gave your heart to Me. . .
The angels sang a song!

"Can you feel My arms around you?
Okay now, listen close.
I know what you are going through.
Be sure, your Daddy knows.

"And you have My full attention
For, no other child on earth
Is more precious, nor more lovable,
Nor represents more worth

"Than you do to your Daddy's heart.
Now, trust Me that it's true.
No other child means more to Me,
Nobody, more than you!

"And it's okay to be a child with Me.
Stop striving to be strong
Be small, be weak, be helplessly
Dependent, that's not wrong!

"You know, when I saw you trying
To be so grown up, I smiled.
Because I came and died to save
Your right to be a Child!"

Mary Campo

An Unseen Hand

It is in the blackest of night that I find my heart,

Adrift on a sea of sadness.

I fear this sorrow will drown me

As it pounds over me, wave after relentless wave.

There is a light on the distant shore

But I am so weary, I have no energy to reach it.

I search for an understanding soul

To swim beside me, urge me on.

In the darkness I hear voices only

Drifting by me, mocking my pain.

It is so cold here — I feel so alone here.

Yet I know there is a Strength much greater than my despair.

He will stay beside me, lift me out of these murky waters,

If only I call on Him. "JESUS!"

I raise my hand, and suddenly there is another,

Holding mine.

Diane M. LeDuc

Showers Of Blessing

It's raining again today, Lord
My dreary mood fits the weather
Like an old threadbare raincoat
Needing to be discarded

The familiar adage:
"April showers bring May flowers"
Tells me to look to a better day —
Yet with restless striving

Your gentle words:
"Cast all your cares on me . . ."
Compel me to commit to you this day —
With trusting relaxation

It's raining again today, Lord
Tossing aside my raincoat
Like a delighted child I'll run headlong into
Your refreshing showers.

Brenda Picazo

Openness

Sharing

Life on the surface only reflects

　　The viewer or the sky.

To see the real stuff,

　　We have to don

Our emotional scubas,

　　And be willing to dive.

Be sure to

　　Delve in awe and wonder,

　　And carry food.

Harpoons scare the real life away.

Betty Reber

the reality
couldn't be more real
give and take
with no fear
or
hesitation
believing
it's safe
knowing
it is
trusting
completely
probing our
minds' limits

not
finding
them

Jolanta B. Uniejewski

Tears On The Inside

It's been a nagging question . . .
                    that I've had for several years
While I search for the answers,
                    only questions reappear.
Can someone find my tears?

So many times I'm paralyzed
                    without finding relief
There's torture and there's pain inside,
                    but tears flee like a thief.

There is this sound my body makes
                    that tries to show the pain.
It mimics whimpers of a child,
                    but seeks for tears in vain.
Inside the ache remains . . .

So where are tears that can't be found?
                    Is it true they do exist?
Could they be just imagined now . . .
                    no matter who insists?

But I do know the pressure in my chest
                    is pain that's real.
Its origin is still unclear
                    and longs to stay concealed.
Hidden tears still unrevealed . . .

[continued]

I'm certain that these tears are there.
                    My heart longs for them so.
For why else would their absence
                    cause the pain inside to grow?

Perhaps the tears are always there
                    just hidden from my eyes
afraid to spill onto my face,
                    revealing my disguise.
The clown-faced lies . . .

But reality is different
                    than glaring self-control.
For all the tears that no one sees
                    have overflowed my soul.

Patty Lane

Visions In Life

Some things I cannot see. Even though my eyes are nearly gone, there are other things that I now see more clearly than ever before.

As the lights grow dim outside, they are illuminated inside of myself. It has been so long since I have seen the unkept corners of my soul; so long without the gift of expression of my own feelings. No more need to rely solely on borrowed words of others to share my thoughts. Hallelujah, a gift is regained! The words once again flow on the paper and dance across the page. Perhaps they stumble and trip a bit, but they are alive and free again! They are mine.

The present moment becomes more cherished. Be aware of yourself, who you are, and what you are doing with your life. Enjoy and be grateful.

[continued]

My eyes may become well and once again see the world. I can only be patient. In return, I have seen a glimpse of my soul and a heightened value for life. Lord, please make this moment last for more than just tonight. Heal me from within. You are the potter and I am the clay. Make me a servant in Thine own precious way.

Jeanne Linnemanstons

Comfort

Come Unto Me

Come, lay your head upon My breast

The epitome of tenderness.

I'll hold you with My strong right arm,

And shield you from the hurt and harm

You feel as through this world you roam

A pilgrim on your journey Home.

I'm always here — if you'll come to Me.

My arms are open — My love is free.

Come, lay your head upon My breast,

And I will give you peace and rest.

"Come unto me, all ye that labour and are

heavy laden, and I will give you rest."

Matthew 11:28 (KJV)

gloria f. parker

Dear Lois

Dear Lois,

Although you cannot hold me I can hold you. In countless ways, I have held you. In great tenderness I quietly, gently made the delicate fabric of my own reflection and gave it to you. You won't remember it. It was before your birth.

Your Mother grieved and shamed of your presence . . . left. But I always had you. You are mine. There is no loss of care or design.

Baby steps I saw. Your first smiles and coos were mine. I was always there. You are mine. Your pudgy legs and chunky arms were cradled in my smile of warm summer sun and gentle wind. Your golden hair was sprinkled from a heavenly diadem and you are mine.

At ease with your growth, but quite unknown to you, an offender crossed your peaceful path and chose to cut you down. In blackest awfulness, I made his frame as well. And he chose to cause the suffocating silent hell.

As you lay paralyzed all my host seemed to stop and gasp in horror at the gaping hollowness that once we called your soul. And you are still mine. Yes, I feel the horror of your pain. I feel the wounds as well. And all the shattered pieces of a fragile little self.

No human touch to ease the pain. No strength to lean upon. Humiliated by sin's worst shame, you were lost and all alone. No words of care, no human comfort for you to trust.

Oh, my dear crushed wounded soul, your despair is mine as well. All my being deeply troubled by the bleakness of your tortured self . . . and you remain mine.

I see it. I feel it. I hear it. I smell it all. It's Me he violates. And you are not alone. Not now . . . not ever. I am there, even though you cannot see me. Trust me to carry you across the threshold of a former self. Trust me to cradle you, to nurture and love you . . . for you will be forever mine.

Lois C. Muhasky

[These words came to the writer while she prayed for understanding of God's presence or lack of it during her abuse. How lovingly our Lord ministered to this wounded heart.]

My Most Precious Creation

I called you. . .
Even though you were told you were an accident — a mistake.
I called you.
I planned and ordained your birth
I created you in your Mother's womb
I knitted your bones together and formed you.
I called you.
When you were wandering in darkness —
I called you.

And you answered . . .
Each time you sought me
You were answering me
Each time you cried for me
You were answering my call
Every time you have called for help
You were answering me
For in your cry you were seeking me for the answer
Which "I Am."

I will never leave you,
I promise.
I will never forsake you,
I promise.
I won't let you go,
I promise.
For in your Heart
In the midst of your turmoil and pain, doubt and fear
You made a choice.
You chose me — The Lord Your God.
And I cherish that choice.
I will protect it and nourish it,
And you.

Every time you fall
I will lift you up with my right hand.
Every time you slip
I will support you
My angels lift you up lest you dash your foot
Against a stone.
You will not be overpowered with evil —
For I am greater within you
You will not be lost —
For I hold you in the palm of my hand
You will not be taken —

For I watch over you with tender jealousy
For I am Your God
Your healer
Your deliverer
Your protector
Your saviour
Your strength
I am here for you
And, I have chosen you.
Even though you feel like you've been riddled with arrows,
I have broken 100 for every 1.
I have kept you and preserved you
I brought you back from the deep void that
sought to swallow you and draw you into
death and darkness —
Even in the depths of despair and depression
Wandering the halls and streets of your illness —
My hand was on you
My angels were around you
My Spirit kept and guided you.

[continued]

Today I walk beside you.
I love you.
I covet you.
You are my child
My child — even though there is still change to come within
I want you to know that I am pleased with you.
And I want you to walk in the promise that
The work I have begun in you —
I will finish.

Last but not least
I want you to know
I forgive you.
Yesterday is past
I must honor my own Word.
Where I command "you" to forgive 70 times 7.
You are forgiven.

Come unto me —
Set aside those "burdens, hurts, painful memories,
And sins" that keep you from me.
Set aside the "guilt"
I do not deny you

You deny me for you are afraid that
These "things" are between us
They are only in your perception of Me —
Allow me to change that.
I desire to comfort you.

Please . . .
Receive my Grace — I died for you
Receive my Peace — my little lamb
Receive my Joy — it is a gift
Receive my Love — as I have yours

My Mercy covers you.

Jesus

Sandra Eldredge

Renaissance House

Renaissance: Reborn, to live again.

I walked into a house one day where lived a friend of mine,
Called to him, searched for him, then waited for a time.
After a while, tried and bored, impatient with the wait,
I stood to leave, quite certain that he had confused the date.

On a table near the door, I saw a note addressed to me. It said:

"Dear friend, I had to leave, my dad has called me home, I
promised him that I'd obey when he first let me roam, It
saddens me that I can't spend the years ahead right here,
We've learned from one another and I'll miss you, that is clear.

The meals we've shared together, the laughter and the tears,
The plans we've made are yours now but, dear one, have no fears.
I'm richer now than when we met, I hope you're richer too,
Perhaps this will bring you comfort. . .

I have willed this house to you."

I sat here stunned and thought about this message given me
I knew my friend was burdened and had longed to be set free.
But how I ached to be with him, traveling by my side,
Until my life was over and my last breath was sighed.

Instead he'd gone and left me here, his father's call was strong,
Could the friend that I called brother have been Jesus all along?

I read the note again:

[continued]

"Dear Friend, I had to leave, my Dad has called me home,
I promised him that I'd obey when He first let me roam,
It saddens me that I can't spend the years ahead right here,
We've learned from one another and I'll miss you, that is clear.

The meals we've shared together, the laughter and the tears,
The plans we've made are yours now but, dear one, have no fears.
I'm richer now than when we met, I hope you're richer too,
Perhaps this will bring comfort . . .

I have willed this House to you."

Janice Gail Knowlton

Analogy Of Love

"Don't you know I love you?"
I heard a small child say.
"Please don't cry any more,
I'll wipe your tears away.
I'll make you laugh and forget your hurts,
just you wait and see."
She gently rocked the old rag doll,
that sat upon her knee.

I never knew why that doll
could mean so much to her.
She had other dolls more costly,
and by far much prettier.
But she loved that doll just as it was,
not new, but torn and tattered.
What ragamuffin appeared to be
did not seem to matter.

I tried replacing that old doll
with dolls that were brand new;
a doll with clean, unmatted hair,
With ALL her limbs, BOTH shoes.
But the child refused, wouldn't give in;
"Doll's my friend," she'd say.
"I'm all she has, and she needs me,
I won't send my friend away."

[continued]

Although it's been some time ago
the memory burns clear,
a loving child whose loyalty laid
with a doll she held so dear.
It reminded me of my (Heavenly) Father's love,
He speaks the same to me —
as the little child spoke to her doll
she rocked upon her knee.

If you need a loving touch today
the Father's hand is near —
To heal the hurts and wounds of life,
because He holds you dear.

Diana Castle

Father, how we thank Thee for the comfort of Thy Word!
Tradition's fallibility could not our spirits gird
With such bright hope, nor could the frail philosophies of men
Give "peace that passeth understanding" and assurance when
Death swiftly calls, and in a fleeting moment takes away
A lovely little part of heaven loaned us for a day.
Not speculation, but our risen Savior's gentle tones:
"Handle me and see, a spirit hath not flesh and bones"
Give us the blessed confidence that when we see His face
The resurrection bodies of those redeemed by grace
Will not be vague, ethereal, but "we shall be like Him";
And though not oft', in longing, our eyes with tears are dim,
One day the dear form and precious pixie face we see no more
We'll see again, and know again, and cherish as before.
And while we wait to share the Joy reunion will afford,
We know that "absent from the body is present with the Lord";
And there is sweet contentment — "He doeth all things well,"
There are no "accidents" with Him.

Dear Father, help us tell
A dying world of Him whose death abolished death and brought
"Life, immortality, to light," and our salvation bought!

Elsie L. Kunert

Permission To Feel

Permission To Feel

I must come to the realization
that
my feelings
are just that . . .
my feelings.

To deny them any longer
is to deny
a part of myself.

Rita McIlwain

Yesterday
I felt
I was
losing it
there
was
this
void
in me
and
I couldn't
name
its
source

I never
paid
attention
to my
feelings
I tried
to ignore,
to distract
myself
from them

it's

NEW

STRANGE

SCARY

to feel
and
experience
feelings
see
how
they
affect me
accept
that
I am
human
allow
myself
to feel
"weak"

Jolanta B. Uniejewski

What
happens
when
the truth
is spoken

nothing
momentous
really

"it's"
not enough
what you're
giving me
I need
you to
talk with
me, to
share
your thoughts
and dreams

there

I

said

it

and

I

still

live

Jolanta B. Uniejewski

three
THE JOURNEY

Now the actual trip begins to take shape. After we survey what will be needed for the healing journey, we must begin in earnest to move toward our destination of wholeness. As we proceed, the map of feelings begins to unfold.

For many, the first stop is *denial / shock*. Initially we think, "This couldn't have happened to me. Sure, it happens to other people, but not to me or my family." We don't want to believe what is coming to light. Every truth faced can seem so unreal, even bizarre. Eventually we come to a point where we begin to accept the reality of our experience, only to fall back into that same denial at other junctures in our recovery process. The emotions expressed in the following poems reveal the difficulty in moving past the denial/shock stage. We need not be discouraged or frightened; this is a natural part of working toward wholeness as we face our past woundedness.

We next encounter *anger*. How many of us are willing to verbalize honestly our anger to God? God knows our hearts. Anger is no surprise to Him. Unfortunately, many of us were taught to bottle our anger rather than address it as a God-given emotion. While God does not condone destructive anger, He does give us permission to release our anger in healthy and appropriate ways. This powerful emotion can destroy many relationships if not resolved. When the anger from abuse or addiction is expressed properly, a great burden is lifted and the resulting freedom enables us to proceed in recovery.

One of the most powerful legs of our journey will be that of *release*. This phase includes feelings of *betrayal*. Poems of betrayal pierce the heart as few can, often being written from the perspective of a small, helpless child. Other poems share the terrible sense of confusion when one who is supposed to love us violates us in some way.

Shame and *doubt* can seem to overwhelm us during the release phase of exploring and expressing our feelings. We believe that somehow we were responsible for what happened to us. We doubt ourselves, our feelings, even our right to be alive. Praise God that He holds us near on this dark path, for unresolved shame and doubt can seem to swallow us in humiliation and despair. The enemy of our soul desires that we be weighted down under such pain and, in the process, be unable to see or hear God. Thankfully, shame and doubt can be overcome and vanquished when each is faced and feelings are allowed to surface.

Most of us on the healing journey travel through *guilt*. We might experience false guilt and blame ourselves for our own hurt and abuse; we might harbor hatred toward the abuser. Many of us suffer from guilt out of our woundedness for we were unable to parent our own children with healthy love. Whatever phases of guilt we must address in our journey, we have permission to feel that deep hurt until we ultimately realize that we can fully give it to our Savior, Who loves us unconditionally.

Loss and *sadness* are experienced when we are ready to recognize *what* we lost as a result of our abuse. Loss of childhood through incest or parental alcoholism, loss of loved ones, loss of hope or dreams, and even loss of desire to continue to heal threaten to overcome us like an ocean wave and wash us out to sea. But this part of our voyage is vital and will finally pass as we face the truth, express the feelings, and reach for God's direction in our lives. David said it well in Psalm 139:7, 9, 10 (ASV):

> Where can I go from Thy Spirit? . . .
> If I . . . dwell in the remotest part of the sea,
> even there Thy hand will lead me . . . .

The final two legs, *acceptance* and *forgiveness*, are extremely difficult passages for abuse survivors. It is important for us to remember, as we read the poetry describing these stages, that the writers aren't condoning what was done to them. The pilgrimage of healing brings a Christian to the time when the painful emotions have been examined, the facts of abuse acknowledged, and the release of pain experienced. Now it is time to accept the reality that this was the life we lived but we can go on because of God's redeeming power and grace.

How He delights in transforming what we describe as trash into treasure! John 16:33 tells us we will have tribulation in this world, but we are to take courage, for Jesus has overcome the world.

Yes, we can go on to *forgive* for His sake. Because He cried out to the Father to forgive His perpetrators of their abuse and violence, we can hold on to Him and ultimately forgive our abusers too. Once again we are like small children who, not knowing how to forgive, reach for His extended hand to help us take those first steps. Countless numbers of survivors have shared forgiveness as one of the most difficult and yet most healing parts of their path to wholeness.

Many of these poems will move you deeply. Through them we become more aware of the ways of wounded hearts and of what will be needed to liberate us from our past bondage. The time has come to walk side by side as both traveler and guest share poetry born out of God's call on the life of each writer. Perhaps you, too, will hear His open invitation to take courage and embrace the healing journey.

Denial / Shock

Scripture Dancer

Seems all my life's been spent in trying

To avoid a world that's real.
Because part of real's the fear and doubt
And pain you've got to feel.

And it didn't take me long to learn,
After being born-again,
That I could even use the Bible
To deny the pain I'm in.

You know you don't feel pain in a black and white world.
You don't have to feel at all.
You just get your Bible and a Strong's Concordance
And you build a great high wall.
But you've got to build it tight
So no doubts can creep in.
(If you're a Scripture dancer
Everything's got an answer
then even if you lose, you win.)

But Jesus wrestled with injustice,
And He felt the pain He saw.
It was the Pharisees who kept denying
There was life beyond the Law.

Their pride kept them from feeling
Even happiness and love.
They missed the peace of just believing,
Had no Hand inside their glove.

[continued]

It's true, you can't feel pain in a black and white world.
You can't even feel at all.
You think you're protected in a safe cocoon,
But you're trapped inside that wall.
You've got it built so tight
That no joy can creep in.
You're a Scripture dancer
Everything's got an answer
(Except how to feel alive again.)

Mary Campo

Your House Or Mine

You were at my door today —

        I pretended you weren't there
                clawing to get out . . .
                              frenzied, wild-eyed.

At the cast iron door; the one designed to protect me,
                    to ward off ancient terrors . . .

I ignored your presence as if my home was calm
                         unruffled.

It's become a strange place — now —
                with its overcrowded emptiness

And you, coexisting in my frantic thoughts
                now crying to be heard,
                      felt,
                        understood.

Yes, you were at my door today
            .

              .

                .
                  pleading to get out.

As I saw your frightened figure there

I realized for the very first time . . .
              the house I've always called my own
                    was never really mine!

Lana Bateman

I'm In The Middle Of A Memory

It couldn't have happened, I must have read it in a book or saw it
in a movie — I'm in the middle of a memory.

He wouldn't have ripped off the pink floral nightie of a little
four-year-old girl.
He couldn't have beat and slapped her face and ears so she
couldn't hear.
I'm sure he didn't pull her hair and laugh.

He couldn't have, I must have read it in a book or saw it in a
movie — I'm in the middle of a memory.

Then why do I hear her screaming "No," "No," "No," "No,"
"No". . . . when he knew and she knew no one was home. And the
room whirled and whirled like an out of control merry-go-round.
And the four-year-old girl stopped screaming and went through
a dark, dark tunnel until she completely disappeared.

It couldn't have happened, I must have read it in a book or
saw it in a movie. I'm in the middle of a memory.

General contributor

The Dark Of Light

If lamps could speak . . .
        I wonder what he'd say

The ancient blind man,
        sitting on the shelf
                hollow eyes fixed in space?

He seems so regal standing there
        draped in royal Chinese robes,
                gnarled staff in hand . . .

Such fine clothes for one who neither sees nor feels,
        who stands vacuously beneath a shade
                and offers us his wares.

What value has this man . . . who holds the lamp?
        His own eternal darkness
                paralyzed in glass;
        His bearded wisdom long beyond expression.

The irony is tragic contradiction
        or comedy in ageless twisted form

That out of his unseeing world —
        my eyes more clearly see,

                and I cannot escape what I despise . . .

                that all too often
                  blindness brings the light.

Lana Bateman

Ripples In A Pond

Vibrations — reverberations

ripples in a pond,

Stand alone on the shore

reaching to beyond.

Searching for a clue

to a story since ingrown,

looking for an answer

to a question yet unknown.

Can the echoes of the past

stir a tragic rhyme,

Or is it lost . . . . forever wandering

through the chambers of my mind?

Kay Kocour

Dress Of Laughter

Beneath her dress of ruffled laughter

She wears a slip of pain

Oh-h-h-h, how sad

her slip is showing

Beneath my dress of ruffled laughter

I, too, wear a slip of pain

N-o-o-o, it cannot be

my slip is showing

I am so ashamed.

Tell me no one sees!

Nancy Kintner

Anger

Anger

I have not dealt with my anger.
It is an emotion I would rarely allow.
Telling myself I had no right —
I would ignore or suppress it.
And I became cold and hard inside.
Only when faced with emotional pain
Did it threaten to break loose in a
Violent, uncontrollable burst.
That's when I would run away so those who
Knew me could not question my feelings or pain.
But I see now the awful truth . . .
I should have been upset as I examined
What has happened to my life.
It would have been better to experience
The anger and hurt instead of letting it
Simmer and stew for so long,
(Occasionally boiling over).
God has been working to clean house in me
. . . And oh, what a mess this room holds!
I am so thankful He knows what is
Needed to let me escape from these
Putrid, stifling, depressing contents.

I could not deal with it
As a child.
I refuse to continue with it
As an adult.
I must finally see this through,
I can no longer run away
Anytime the pain becomes too great.
With God's help I will learn to
Stay and face the truth . . .
To face myself . . .

Jo Winkowitsch

I Still Need You

Please dear Lord
   don't turn your back
Please dear Lord
         please . . .
           hold me still.
Like an angry child
I still need you.
Even when I yell "I hate you."
     I hold my arms open wide
        to only you.

Lois C. Muhasky

Boundaries

Boundaries are not visible
they lurk within your being — their voices heard only when
violated.

I guess since the boundaries are invisible,
one must learn how to point them out without ripping off
someone's head. It would seem prudent to develop skills
that say "go no further," "you're on risky ground." Some will
respect — some will stumble on.

Boundaries are not walls — they are fleshy tables of the heart —
gorged with the blood of life and must be protected verbally.

I always assume that people have some sort of inborn radar or
ability to know when they're close or have crossed into the red
zone.

They do not.

Kay Kocour

DIS-
ILLUSIONED
I
STILL
TRY,
I
TRY
TO
BUILD
A RELATION-
SHIP
AND
THE
DRAMA
IN
MY
LIFE
IS
NO
LESS
THAN
IN
THE
GREEK
THEATRE
IT
SEEMS
LIKE
I'M
ON A
STAGE
AND
DON'T
KNOW
ANYMORE
IF

MY
FEELINGS
(NUMBED
FOR
SO
LONG)
ARE
REAL
OR
ARTIFICIAL
AT
THAT
MOMENT
THE
SAFEST
WAY
OUT
IS
GOING
INTO
A RAGE . . .

Jolanta B. Uniejewski

Anatomical Jigsaw

With no arms how can I take your hand

no legs run the race

with shattered heart love my neighbor

merciful God . . . hear my case.

With no voice how can I sing your praise

no ears hear the sea

with ingrown eyes see the sunshine

relate emotionally.

Gall of anger well up and out

oh would that it were done!

. . . . I'd gladly give you a piece of my mind

but alas, I haven't one.

Kay Kocour

The Poison Tree

I was angry with my friend
I told him so . . .
and it did end.

I was angry with a foe
I told her not . . .
and it did grow

. . . day by day with my fears
night by night with my tears.

Till it bore an apple bright.
So I picked it with all my might
and as I ate with a stealthy grin,

it began to eat me . . .

from within!

Jim Kocour

Release: Betrayal

Weekend With Daddy

Flying kites

fishing in a lake so clear

look . . . you can see the hook,

basketball, kick the can,

reading again the favorite book.

A few beers with the boys

what can it hurt,

mom's not even here

but suddenly a shroud surrounds

shame's own atmosphere

And the hot breath of evil's passion

cannot be restrained

and daddy's little girl

will never be the same . . . .

                        neither will daddy.

                        General contributor

Betrayal

A careless word tossed thoughtlessly
finds its way back into an ear
never meant to hear.

Actions undefinable — inconceivable
who is left . . . . what is left?

Trust lies crushed

a heart once aglow with promise now smolders,
self consumed.

I pick through the ashes
and come upon a charm of some sort —
its chain undamaged.

I place it around my neck and glance at its inscription.

"BETRAY ME"

I rip it from my neck
heave it as far as my strength
and in the other direction, as far as far is . . .
I make my home.

It's lonely sometimes but it's safe.

Kay Kocour

What Is A Daddy?

What is a daddy?
    That's silly to ask.
For everyone knows
    He has dutiful tasks.

A part of our birth,
    He's there from the start.
But his role isn't clear
    After he's done that part.

Each one though different
    still works out his role.
Some may try to comfort
    While others control.

Theirs is the power
    in the homes where they rule.
There's power to encourage . . .
    though some ridicule.

What is a daddy
    to a small helpless child?
And what of the man
    whose own girl he defiles?

What is a daddy
    to that sweet little girl?
Is it someone to love
    through the insults he hurls?

[continued]

Does she really need
  such a father around?
And must she still love him
  as if duty-bound?

So maybe he's right.
  What he says is O.K.
If he causes her pain
  it's her price to pay.

Her heart wants much more.
  Could that need be so wrong?
To long for a daddy
  that's both loving and strong?

His touch should speak truth
  that she's safe in his care?
For he'd always protect her
  as special and rare . . .

But that's just a dream
  for this little child
Who lived with a dad
  who destroyed as he smiled

General contributor

Drunk Again

Staggering tonight . . .
The arguments that fill each room,
   a waking child in fright.

   Baby still asleep . . .
While babbled screams drone on.
   Oh, who will stop
         this murderous theme
            before each child is grown?

Can no one hear the cries?
Of children draped in fear?
  And where's the prince
      who dragon slays?
         Oh God, let him be near!

Lana Bateman

Where Were You

You robbed me once
   when I was just a child
      and had no understanding of this life.
         I lost my right to live because you left.
            You danced and played
               while devils filled my nights.

You were the parents
   that I felt were gods
      and all you did was surely right for me —
         but where were you
            when darkness cut me down
               and helplessness descended like the sea?

I wish that you had heard my agony
   when stories flowed of terror,
      scary nights
         but you were gone . . .
            Then laughed at all I said . . . .

     " A child's imagination."

A foolish child imagines . . .

               death-filled sights?? . . .

               General contributor

Release: Shame / Doubt

Nightmares

When will all of
the nightmares end?
When at last can I
call myself friend?

Attacked by one
trusted to care —
I lie here alone,
while no one's there.

Swallowed feelings,
deep searing pain,
I never can be . . .
the same again.

Jesus reach down,
hold "little Eve" tight,
through all those long
and empty nights.

Give her blessings
from far above . . .
then wrap her gently
in Your great love.

Eve Bailey
(written about Eve and her inner child)

My Shame

Dear God,
    I can't get clean . . .
        no matter how I scrub my dirty skin.

           Not even soap can
                take away my shame . . .
                    or bring back gentle innocence again.

I look about me . . .
    wondering who knows.

           If just by looking
                all the world can see . . .
                    the emptiness that once
                        was called my soul . . .
                          before those filthy hands
                          were touching me.

Oh Lord,
    It hurts me still . . .
        though years have passed
            since you have touched my heart
            and changed my name.

           For even though
                my life has been made new . . .
                Why Father, can't you
                    take away the shame?

Lana Bateman

Shame

Shame   Shame   Shame

who's to blame
who's to blame

My soul wilts from guilt and shame

who's to blame
who's to blame

My heart — a mask . . . . melts like wax
My mind — a muddle of rubble and trouble
Anguish of spirit languished in pain

who's to blame
who's to blame

Who will null the sorrow — the shame
Who can dull my screams of pain
Terror by night — arrow by day

who'll take the blame
who'll take the blame

If you are willing . . . . you can ease my pain
If you are willing . . . . you can bear the shame

I always wondered . . . . was it meet to die,
A look at my life now tells me why . . . .

And so He was led to Calvary's Tree
A blameless man to die for me.
For what grand purpose
Can anyone see?
To set me free . . . . to set me free.

Because He loves me . . . .
He sets me free.

Kay Kocour

Release: Guilt

Beyond The Door

I was judged guilty without a trial

banished for being a child . . .

helpless child.

You closed the door on me,

sealed the door emotionlessly and

as I turn around, I see my cell of isolation

barred, empty and cold.

And the years pass.

Then in a dream, the door opened wide

and as I sprang to greet my freedom,

to my horror I find you inside,

inside the adjoining cell,

barred, empty and cold.

For, it seems you too were judged guilty without a trial

banished for being a child . . .

helpless child.

Kay Kocour

In Times Like These

When I see my children failing at life,
over and over again;

anxiety and sorrow well to such levels,
I wish that all could end.

In times like these, I go again
to Calvary and pause
and wonder what Mary felt
as she saw her son hanging on The Cross.

In some way did she think she'd failed,
or did she know it was in God's plan
to take The Son of Man so violently
from this sinful land?

Now that I've written these things down
my heart is saddened to see
my old nemesis, pride,
surfacing in me
and suggesting that if I've failed,
I somehow had control
of the lives You have given to me
perhaps authority over their souls.

Now, I'm sorry for my faithlessness
and give back everything I am;
Mother, daughter, sister, teacher,
administrator, friend.

I give it all to You, Lord,
so in me You'll be glorified
and in my life remaining,
I might be satisfied.

Kay Kocour

To my angel up in heaven

for you I've shed so many tears,

for the pain and heartache caused

and the lonely missing years . . .

I can never fully say

what's so deep within my heart,

or how badly that I feel

and how I wish we weren't apart.

Please forgive me my dear son

for my dastardly past crime,

oh, but how I thank the Lord

we'll be together in His time.

Bobbie Jo Mullet
(in memory of Benjamin Andrew)

Release: Loss / Sadness

A Child's Song

I can remember the sound of my feet
As I shuffled along the walk,

And the look on my mother's face
When she never had time to talk.

I can almost hear the sound of my voice
Singing alone in that tree,

And I often recall my father's "good-night"
As he passed, never touching me.

Sing a child-alone song
Sing a dusty rhyme,
Sing a childhood-blue song
Sing of long lost time.

I can remember the day that she died
It was quiet and I was alone,

And I still recall the thoughts that I had
Of a mother I'd never known.

No, we never quite reached for each other
So few were the things we shared.

Where in the world
could those lost years have gone
And why hadn't anyone cared?

Sing an all-alone song
Eyes are filled with tears,
Sing a sad-but-true song
And weep for wasted years.

Lana Bateman

Variations

There are four kinds of kids:

one pulls wings from butterflies,

another cries when it happens,

a third runs and tells

while the last turns her back,

outwardly ignores the scene but

inwardly grieves for the rest of her life.

Kay Kocour

Butterfly Wings

I sat in a therapist's office today
    surrounded by books on children
        and boxes heaped with toys.

Above the couch hung two pictures,
    each softly beckoning you
        to the wonders of a child's world.

Tiny little fingers reaching for butterfly wings
    faces filled with awe and delight.

It seemed somehow surreal to see them there . . .
    as if to show a purity that seldom exists . . .
        . . . apart from pictures.

If only children's eyes could stay so trusting,
        tender,
            unafraid.

And chubby hands remain so undefiled
    save by dust from butterfly wings

But in this abscessed world
    where lives survive
        while feelings lie entombed.

There's little place for graceful memorials . . .
        even
            to
                the death of
                  innocence.

Lana Bateman

To My Unborn Child

Such a beautiful baby you would have been!
    Soft and silky —dimpled chin.
A Stephanie or Benjamin?
    We'll never know — you never came.

Attentive to my voice — my touch;
    And oh, my God, loved so much!
Responsive, alert, intelligent mind —
    A gift from God, one of a kind.

And what of your coloring?
    Your hair? Your eyes?
Brown like his — or blue as the skies?
    We'll never know — you never came.

Oh, it doesn't matter, I realize,
    You would have been a gorgeous surprise!
Your very own person — a unique creation,
    Unlike any child I can imagine.

I've missed you terribly through the years.
    Your nonexistence found birth in tears.
Tears for you whom I never carried,
    Even though for a time I was married.

An empty womb — no babe at my breast
    Searching for milk and warmth and rest.
A heartache I bear that will never be gone;
    Flesh of my flesh, bone of my bone,
My own, my own, my very own —
    But you never came.

gloria f. parker

Loss

Raging waves
   seek out my sun-scorched shore.

They come and go like uninvited guests
   whose silent messages unfurl with brutal force . . .

      then quietly fade back into the sea.

Disappearing like disinterested bystanders . . .

   leaving nothing behind

      save

        fingerlike trails

         of sparkling foam.

Reminders of uniquely spilled vulnerabilities . . .

      long . . .

       long . . .

        ago.

Lana Bateman

Lost In Time

Some babies live in holes . . .
    dark recesses in the cold earth
        where the first terrifying screams and tears . . .
            melt into panic, quick frozen into silence.

"Don't scream, don't cry, don't breathe . . ."
    an endless message acted out
    to render innocence too helpless and afraid to feel
            experience
               or taste of life.

Years pass, body grows and mind becomes the season.
        A puppet takes the lighted stage.

But in the deepest places of the heart
        a baby's tears still fall without a sound
While all the dreams of joy and love are lost
        nor can the buried anger bridge the gap.

For those condemned to holes are living dead,
    prepared for death before they've ever lived
        Within that deep black pit — too small to move
        the best of life departs a fragile soul.

And all that ever hopes or yearns to be,
        is frozen into silence
            lost in time.

General contributor

Baby Grace

Did she feel the doctor's knife . . .
         that cut her deep within?
Or simply pass from womb to death
         destroyed by mortal's whim?

But what about the heart and soul
         of this lost little one?
Could hands that held the knife that day . . .
         not see the damage done?

Where was God in this young life
         could He not see her pain?
He could have stopped it all you say
         but chose not to sustain.

I know that God is sovereign
         for He says He's everywhere.
So where was He that long dark day
         when innocence laid bare?

They had no right to take her life
         but did it anyway.
Placed upon the altar . . .
         she's the one who had to pay.

The doctors couldn't value her
         for cash they took her life.
Her mom and dad were in the room
         but left her to the knife!
And where do doctors bury
         these fragile lives denied?

The grave, a dirty trash bin . . .
                          awaited her outside.
            A wasted life . . .
                  does no one care . . .
                        not cherished,
                              loved,
                                    or touched.

A soul eternal left this world
                  a gentle life lay crushed!

                        General contributor

A Christmas Rose

What is the holiday without your smile . . .
      the sound your laughter makes
            with sparkling eyes?
And joy that once had filled your every room
      now wilted like a rose that blooms and dies.

The house so strangely silent empty stands . . .
      a thundering quiet
            shouts you are not there.
While others take the things that once were yours
      and memories bring tears too great to bear.

I wish that I could hear your voice again . . .
      and sing the songs
            that filled our last brief hours
When arms wrapped round my neck spoke of your love
      and strong oak shrank in time to gentle flower.

I've longed for those late nights and things we shared,
      thoughts of your childhood
            silly pranks you tried.
The day you jumped off of your Grandma's roof
      and found that Mary Poppins, too, had lied.

No, longing for your face won't make it come;
      your voice is quiet still,
            no laugh remains . . .
And no one fills your place, my own sweet friend.
      My Christmas rose can never bloom again.

But in the highest heaven, songs are heard.
      The voices of the kingdom
            worship blend . . .
A tiny babe was born that blessed day . . .
      And now my Christmas rose blooms just for Him!

Lana Bateman

Death

You speak of death, I know her well,

she has stalked my family and claimed

my son. In her shadow now, I must live

day and night, such pain, such sorrow.

She is forever with me, there is no

forgetfulness, no rest, no peace. Oh

Lord, my God where do I go from here?

Roxie Adair

Joy Comes In The Morning

My tears are endless — night and day;

How can I keep on existing this way?

Is there no balm — no salve for this wound?

So many I've loved to death have succumbed.

The sky is grey — the earth is frozen;

God has taken those He's chosen.

Is there no balm — no salve for this wound?

So many I've loved to death have succumbed.

When springtime comes will this pain become lighter?

How many more months can I be a "fighter?"

Is there no balm — no salve for this wound?

So many I've loved to death have succumbed.

When Christ arose that Easter day,

He tore the bars of death away!

Yes! There is balm — there is healing in sight;

For He Who arose turned the darkness to light!

He conquered death and rose again —

Death, our enemy, cannot win.

Over this sorrow I'll be victorious

Because of His Resurrection glorious!

gloria f. parker

To Grieve

It's not the big things so much
Holidays, graduations, weddings
We've toughed them all
But, the color yellow, pepper, a flower,
    a song, the wind, the rain, a sunny
    day, a dog barking
Out of nowhere your heart stands still,
    filled with the memories and the longing.
Life must be lived, work to be done, laughter to be sought.
To grieve is to love, to remember,
    to long for, to cherish.
To grieve is to have known a great love,
    a gentle love, a sweet love.
I do grieve so.

Nancy B. Quinn

Where'd The Time Go?

Daddy, Happy Father's Day!
Gee, you look nice in that tie.
Think the Yankees'll win the pennant?
My, the weather's sure been dry.

Me? Oh yeah, I'm doing fine.
No, there isn't much that's new.
Except I've, I've been thinking lately
That I'd really like to talk with you.

Oh Daddy, where'd the time go?
How'd so many years get by
Before I sensed this long-hushed yearning
and heard the child in me cry:

"Daddy hold me, Daddy love me.
Daddy own me with your smile.
Daddy tell me you're so happy
That I am your special child."

Oh Daddy, life's so short and
How we while away the years
Making small talk, taking cat walks
Over feelings, hopes and fears.

And Daddy is it too late
To uncover how we feel?
Have we gone this way too long
To take a chance at being real?

What is it that constrains us?
Is it stubborn family pride?
Do you wish you'd said this to **your** dad?
Had your father's father cried:

[continued]

"Daddy hold me,
Daddy love me.
Daddy own me with your smile.
Daddy tell me you're so happy
That I am your special child."

And now the years pass swiftly.
And the seasons race away.
We've no promise of tomorrow,
But God's given us today.

Do Daddy, please come closer.
I just can't quite seem to touch
That place in you that holds the love
That we both need so much.

And Daddy please don't leave me
Before you can take me there.
Where your softest self stays hidden
And my guarded heart lies bare.

"Daddy Hold me, Daddy love me.
Daddy own me with your smile.
Daddy tell me you're so happy
That I am your special child."

Mary Campo

Dad's Watch

Every day I take it out

And wind it just once more;

But I'd rather have you here with me

To wear it as before.

gloria f. parker

I had a little baby that I never got to hold

She only made it halfway to her birth (a girl, we're told)

After I was prepped and set for her delivery,

They didn't bring her, wrapped snug and warm for Chris and me to see.

Instead, God took her home while she was still inside of me.

She died while she was growing — they say those babies don't count,

But she sure did make a difference in our lives without a doubt.

She helped us to see this life with a different perspective

To grow up and to give our lives a whole new directive.

She helped us care for each other and our friends a little more . . .

. . . Quite a job for one, they say, who was never even born.

She was "extracted," then "disposed of" . . .

. . . the terms sound awfully cruel

but God was right there with us — us and our little girl.

For the body didn't matter, when God took her spirit then

But she'll live in us forever till in heaven, we meet again.

Patricia Wedertz

A Letter To The Baby I Lost

Dear Little One,

It is with broken heart I write to you . . . . I see your little hands that will never grasp my own. I can almost feel your tender form that I yearn to hold so close. Overpowering pain and sorrow draw close to me through my loss of you.

What color is your hair . . . your eyes? What makes you laugh . . . or cry? Did you know you had three sisters and a brother? If only I could have kissed you good-bye then maybe I wouldn't hurt so bad. O deepest misery . . . I feel like a moving grave, a desolate parched desert where the wind has blown my tenderest flower away.

And so through death you have entered another life where you shall never know the pain of sin or be touched by sin's dire consequence.

You have found your rest, your eternal cradle where your eyes will sparkle and your laughter echo throughout all of Heaven's palace.

Dear Heavenly Father kiss my baby and stroke her hair, hold her close to you . . . tell her, "I love her."

Lois C. Muhasky

Acceptance

His Designs

Shine your light on this

    loss, Lord.

With your illumination,

    I see it

        not as pain,

        not as grief,

But as a single thread in your design,

    Beautiful color

        silver,

        or golden,

intricately woven into the

    fabric of my life.

Edith Martin

Child Of Mine

I'M JUST A POOR DYSFUNCTUAL,
THAT'S WHY I CAN'T BE PUNCTUAL.
I'VE BEEN ABUSED AND CAN'T THINK STRAIGHT, YOU SEE.

MY LIFE WAS HARD, MY CHILDHOOD MARRED,
AND MY LITTLE PSYCHE JARRED,
WHEN DADDY YELLED AT MOM WHEN I WAS THREE.

YOU JUST DON'T KNOW THE PAIN I'VE HAD!
MY MAMA TOLD ME I WAS BAD,
THE TIME I ACCIDENTALLY SPILLED HER BEER.

MY TEDDY BEAR GOT THROWN AWAY
ONE DAY WHEN I WENT OUT TO PLAY...
THERE'S HARDLY ANY HOPE FOR ME, I FEAR.

BUT WAIT! YOU SAY THAT JESUS CAME
SO HE COULD TAKE ALL OF MY SHAME,
AND GIVE ME JOY AND LIFE ABUNDANTLY?

I'LL TAKE IT... WOW! THAT'S QUITE A TRADE
THAT JESUS, ON THE CROSS, HAS MADE!
I'M HIS! HE'S MINE! FOR ALL ETERNITY!!
HE'S SET ME FREE! HE'S SET ME FREE!

BUT.....

THEY SAY I'M CODEPENDENT, TOO,
AND I SUPPOSE THAT COULD BE TRUE,
ALTHOUGH I ONLY TRY TO KEEP THE PEACE.

HOW COULD YOU BLAME POOR ME FOR THAT?
IF HE WEREN'T SUCH A DIRTY RAT
WE'D ALL BE HAPPY, AND MY JOB COULD CEASE!

YOU SAY THAT JESUS WANTS HIM, TOO?
MY HUSBAND, KIDS, THE WHOLE DARN CREW?
OK WITH ME . . . (IS THIS TOO GOOD TO LAST?)

I ONLY TRUST, THAT'S ALL I DO?
AND LEAVE THE REST, LORD, UP TO YOU?
HURRAY! MY CODEPENDENCY IS PAST!!
AT LONG, LONG, LAST! AT LONG, LONG, LAST?

OH, PLEASE, DEAR JESUS, HELP ME GROW,
AND LEARN THE THINGS I NEED TO KNOW,
SO I MAY HEAL AND CHANGE TO BE LIKE YOU.

SO I CAN LEAVE THE PAST BEHIND,
BE SELDOM BLUE, AND MOSTLY KIND,
AND FIND YOUR PROMISES ALL TO BE TRUE.
I'LL FOLLOW YOU! I'LL FOLLOW YOU!

". . . but one thing I do: forgetting what lies behind and reaching
forward to what lies ahead, I press on toward the goal for the
prize of the upward call of God in Christ Jesus."
Philippians 3:13,14 (NASV)

OF COURSE I KNOW IT'S NOT THAT FAST
ONE COMES TO GRIPS WITH ALL THINGS PAST;
BUT WHO I AM IN CHRIST IS WHAT I'VE LEARNED.

AS I REPLACE A LIE WITH TRUTH
THAT'S IN HIS WORD, I'M GIVEN PROOF,
HE'S ALL THE THINGS FOR WHICH I'VE EVER YEARNED!

IT'S BEEN SO HARD FOR ME TO FEEL
EMOTIONS, AND BE REALLY REAL . . . . . .
ALTHOUGH I'VE NOT ARRIVED, I'VE COME QUITE FAR.

SO NOW WHEN I SEE YOU, MY FRIEND,
AND SENSE YOUR HOPE IS AT ITS END,
I KNOW THAT I CAN LOVE YOU AS YOU ARE.

[continued]

THE ROAD'S BEEN LONG, IT'S NOT BEEN SHORT,
AND THERE'VE BEEN TIMES WHEN I'D ABORT
GOD'S HAND OF DISCIPLINE UPON MY LIFE.

BUT HE'S LOVED ME, AND NOT LET GO:
HE'S HELD ME AS I'VE TRIED TO GROW
INTO A CALMER, LOVING MOM AND WIFE.

AS I HAVE READ HIS WORD, HE'S TALKED
TO ME; AND I GOT UP AND WALKED,
AND SOON BEGAN TO RECOGNIZE HIS VOICE.

THE CHANGE HAS BEEN SO GRADUAL,
AS I HAVE YIELDED TO HIS PULL
TO GIVE HIM ALL . . . . . BUT I HAVE MADE MY CHOICE!
AND I REJOICE! AND I REJOICE!

HE LOVES ME UNEQUIVOCALLY;
HIS TRUTH INSIDE HAS SET ME FREE,
TO WORSHIP, AND TO TRUST HIM, RAIN OR SHINE.

AND WHEN I SEE HIM FACE TO FACE,
AND SEE BEYOND THIS EARTHLY PLACE,
I'LL HEAR, "YOU ARE MY TREASURE, CHILD OF MINE."
O JOY SUBLIME . . . O JOY SUBLIME . . .

"Now therefore, if you will obey my voice and keep my
covenant, then ye shall be a peculiar treasure unto me above all
people: for all the earth *is* mine." *Exodus 19:5* (KJV)

Alyson Fry

The Child Inside

IT'S SO HARD FOR ME TO SAY HOW I FEEL
FOR I'VE BEEN ASLEEP FOR YEARS.
AND NOW YOU ASK ME TO OPEN MY EYES.
AND SHARE WITH YOU MY FEARS?

WHY DID YOU LEAVE ME WENDY?
I NEEDED MORE TIME TO PLAY
MORE TIME TO ROCK MY BABY DOLLS,
BUT YOU TOOK THAT ALL AWAY.

I TURNED AROUND AND YOU WERE GONE
YOU LEFT WITHOUT A TRACE
YOU LEFT WITHOUT A KISS GOODBYE
THAT HURT IS HARD TO ERASE.

I'M SCARED AND AFRAID TO TRUST YOU
FOR I'LL FEEL THE PAIN INSIDE
THE DAY YOU LEFT ME STANDING ALONE
WAS THE DAY THAT LITTLE GIRL DIED.

I WANT TO RUN AND MEET YOU.
TO STAND CLOSE BY YOUR SIDE
FOR YOU TO HOLD AND LOVE ME AGAIN
BUT A PART OF ME STILL WANTS TO HIDE.

WE NEED TO BE TOGETHER.
TO FEEL EACH OTHER'S PAIN
WORKING TO PUT IT BEHIND US
TO FORGIVE AND NOT TO BLAME.

THE ROAD AHEAD WON'T BE EASY
BUT WE'LL RISE WITH THE MORNING SUN
TO LEARN TO LOVE EACH OTHER.
AND TO LEARN TO LIVE AS ONE.

Wendy Petry

Integration

When I am in your presence, my mind and heart are one.

I am content.

Then I am reminded of what it took, the years, the tears,

and I am strengthened to know if this is possible, then

nothing is impossible.

Although I am saddened because of what might have been,

I am buoyed because of what is . . . for that is all that

really matters to me now.

If I am new because of all we are together, then, as one,

we can relate to another as a whole.

Since I am, you are and we will ever be . . .

and if this makes any sense whatsoever,

please explain it to me.

Kay Kocour

Dear Encourager

Tonight in your speech on incest recovery
You were confident, with a gleam in your eye,
When you declared if it weren't for my woes
There'd be little strength inside.

Now how can goodness be spawned from evil
And devastation bear life?
No matter how hard I try to imagine,
This thought brings only strife.

I think I know what you meant to say
How good all this turned out to be.
But friend, 'twas the healing from God, not sin,
That rescued and transformed me!

(Miah) Ann Hotchkiss

Candle On The Water

There's a time to be a light
shining from the shore
instead of being swallowed by the sea.

A time to step aside
nursing my own wounds
instead of plunging in where I would be

another drowning victim
joining all the others
lost forever on the ocean floor.

There's a time to be a lighthouse
showing by example
one can finally reach the exit door.

The exit from the hell
we lived in all those years —
an entrance to a better life on earth.

The door that I passed through
can open up for you —
and everything it cost me

— it was worth!

Janice Gail Knowlton

Forgiveness

I Forgive

I forgive you for the lonely nights
                you left me with the maid
And trusted her to keep me safe
                while you went out and played.

I wish that you had loved me
                and protected me those nights.
The anger then would fade away . . .
                your presence could bring light.

But since we can't go back in time
                and change the lives we lived,
I reach now to my Jesus
                and He cries out, "Child forgive."

"For you can't know the agony
                I felt upon the cross
But, you, like Me will learn to see
                what's painful can't be lost.

So once you've vented anger
                and betrayals you have known,
Your wounded heart will find its rest
                all sin is now atoned.

Yes, you can feel forgiveness,
                just as I've felt it for you,
They, too, are crippled children
                and they know not what they do."

General contributor

Sorry

"I'm sorry," he said, and walked away,

His debt too great for him to pay.

What good would that do for the grief he had brought?

Yet what else could he say to the tears in my heart?

My sins are so great, Lord, how can I pay

For the grief I have given You day after day?

How Your heart, Lord has cried! But for my sins You died —

And for his sins. He's sorry. Throw Your arms open wide,

For I know You are willing to hold him to You.

Draw me close in Your other arm, Lord — I'm sorry, too.

M. I. Martin

How Can I Know?

I was the child you expected to fail.
    Something about me was lazy or dull
        or maybe I didn't fit in the family.

There never was a really rebellious time.
    Although I felt my heart grow hard inside
        and often hated you for not loving me.

Still, I did what you asked of me.
    For the most part, I tried to be good
        though sometimes I just closed my ears.

I never found out how to please you,
    what it would take to make you talk
        or just tell me what you wanted.

I'm sorry that I disappointed you.
    Could it be that you will never know
        how I longed to make you proud?

When I knelt to pray tonight, I wept.
    You couldn't understand the child I was.
        But how can I withhold my love from you today?

For I will never know the child you were.

Lana Bateman

Running On Empty

I could forgive and forget
Without too much trouble,
After I'd been sufficiently
Apologized to.
But, when the person who wronged me
Was ignorant of that fact,
Or didn't care . . .
. . . THEN forgiveness came hard.

I thought of Christ —
— Horribly fixed upon a cross,
(Though innocent of any crime).
Forgiving those who hated Him,
Those who denied Him, and,
(Most miraculous of all),
Forgiving those of us who
Put Him there.

Then I felt His love renewing me
And overflowing to cover
Those around me . . . washing away
My black hurt and bitter anger.
Though my forgiveness may be in
Short supply, I don't have to
Wait in line for more.
The pump NEVER runs dry at the
Filling station of the Lord.

Jo Winkowitsch

Forgiveness

Expressing emotion

Letting go of the story

Giving up my right to hurt back

I want to be whole

Jesus cleanse my soul and

Unchain me at last from my past.

Kay Kocour

New Life

Desire the life that inspires

Recite the verse that heals

Forgiven wrongs will reflect

New life! ! ! ! ! ! !

Lloyd H. Thomas, Sr.

four

OBSTACLES

I just spent an evening with a young woman who had read my previous book, *Bible Promises for the Healing Journey*. She said, "I wish I could say that I spend most of my time in the section called Rewards, but it wouldn't be true." She shared that she reached for the book every night and always found herself in the chapter, *Obstacles*.

Isn't that true of most of us? We long to go straight to the rewards, sidestepping the journey with its obstacles. If you are already on the path to emotional freedom, then you are familiar with the conflicts that come and can identify with many of the struggles dealt with by our writers.

As I shared some of these poems with several groups of victims in recovery, I heard voices all over the room whispering, "Yes, yes, yes." They knew at last they were not alone in their trauma and pain. They were not emotional outcasts, but believers who by God's grace had begun to face the truth so long denied.

Times of *discouragement* will never be easy, but how much more bearable when we know others have walked the same road. As we see God's victory in their lives, we are comforted by their examples.

If *pride* is one of your areas of struggle, you are not alone. The poems addressing pride describe how self-reliant we can become when we reach a point where we think we no longer need God or further healing. Total recovery is not instant; it takes place all the way to heaven.

Compromise is a subtle enemy and our response to it can be seen in two ways. We may refuse to compromise when mediation could benefit our healing process or we may make unhealthy compromises. Either way, compromise is an obstacle that must be addressed.

Even the most goal-oriented Christians, while dealing with recovery, will experience times of *aimlessness*. When the old structures of dysfunction are dismantled, and reconstruction begins, there are intervals of wondering.We wonder if we can make sense out of all that has happened. We wonder who we are now, if the pain is worth it, if we will get better. These are all natural responses and part of shock and denial that continue to reappear in our course of travel.

Ridicule and *rejection* often go hand in hand. We must become vulnerable to share openly about the many ways we experienced ridicule and rejection as children. For most, our current relationships are also affected by these same dynamics.

Can a Christian suffer *unbelief?* Abuse victims who have come to Christ can answer that question easily. In the midst of the darkest moments of one's memories, it is hard to believe in a loving, caring God. As Jesus felt forsaken, so do those who have known great abuse. But those who persevere through their hurt and times of despair, and continue to seek God, will feel His all-encompassing arms and His gentle touch.

We hunger for immediate gratification. We want the answers before the questions are asked. *Impatience* earmarks our nation and generation. The poetry of this section shows that the healing process is not immune to that same striving. We want to be whole *now!* We are not so interested in the Great Physician as we are the great magician. Why doesn't God move more quickly, or why aren't we there yet? Few in recovery have escaped encounters with this adversary.

Hopelessness overshadows us when we feel there is no reason to go on, no way out, and no answers for our deepest needs. It is so freeing to stop pretending and be honest with God when we feel this turmoil. Our journey to completion in Him will include awareness that we are capable of feeling hopeless, even though we know He cannot abandon us.

I've spoken to many people at conferences, retreats, and seminars throughout the years. Never have I counseled with so many people who don't know how to trust. *Mistrust* is as rampant in the church body as it is in our culture. Wives describe a lack of communication and fear of rejection in relationships with husbands. Some staff members in churches are uneasy about sharing their true concerns lest their jobs be put on the line. The list is endless.

How much more difficult is trust for those who, for example, have suffered child abuse at the hands of their caretakers! These poems are powerful indeed. Maya Angelou once said, "One act of sexual abuse takes a child from the innocence of knowing nothing to the cynicism of believing nothing!" That one statement describes the depth of mistrust an abuse victim must overcome.

Temporary relief attracts many who reach for emotional freedom. It is easy to stop short of recovery because we momentarily feel better. Sadly, we eventually become acutely aware that we have not yet finished the course.

Why isn't it over? Why must we go on? Why me? *Self-pity* can be a time-consuming and energy-draining detour.

If only we knew who we were. If only we had value. If only we could belong. If only there were guarantees that those we love wouldn't leave us. These are some of the thoughts that plague us when we face feelings of *unworthiness*. While most of us accept that we are worthy in Christ, our past abuse sends a different emotional message. Soul growth helps to uncover the truth of what we feel, while erasing the lie that we have to feel forever unworthy.

Fear can paralyze us and delay our progress to recovery. Some fear the first steps of the journey. Some fear being unable to escape present symptoms of past pain, while others fear self-destruction if the truth is brought to light. Ultimately we are apprehensive about all the pieces of our lives falling apart and we wonder who can ever put them back together again. These are just a few of the most common anxieties as we travel through abusive memories and learn to accept our past.

Last, but critically important, is the journeyer's battle with *loneliness* and *isolation*. Our poems share the loneliness and isolation that may stalk the pilgrim who desires reality and honesty in relationships. When we have been deeply wounded, it becomes easy to disappear into ourselves and not be a part of what is happening around us. We complain that we are lonely, only to retreat in isolation if someone tries to come near. A place of comfort will open as you can identify with others. Many have gone before you, some are right where you are today, and others will come along behind you. *You are not alone.*

You are brave and courageous, for in spite of all of the obstacles, you have chosen to take His hand and make the healing journey. Your Shepherd will not fail you no matter where the journey may take you. No hindrance is so severe, no loss so great, that He cannot lead you through. His open arms are always there surrounding you with His lovingkindness and compassion.

No matter what obstacles you encounter, He will never desert or forsake you *(Hebrews 13:5c)*. In spite of all the world and its sin, He still calls you "the joy of His heart." Praise God! There is now no condemnation for those who are in Christ Jesus! *(Romans 8:2)*

Discouragement

Delays

Lord, it seems I've hit a wall
Of hopes and dreams deferred
The blessings you have promised me
All throughout your word
The things I've long believed were mine
And took for granted are
Now not in view and seem to be
Away — so very far

But, Lord, today you brought to mind
How Joseph's dreams came true
Not in ways he may have thought
Or the times that he would choose
Delays, they must have plagued his mind
And tempted him to doubt
Your love and wisdom — the whole way
You in his life came out
But in the end his life displayed
The perfect Master–plan
The finished gem a diamond rare
Not made by any man

So, Lord, though I am feeling now
So loose, at odds, undone
I know these days will bring to me
The life planned from "day one"
Delays, yes, Lord, they're
hard to bear
And dreams deferred wear thin
But you're the God of hopes fulfilled
Who ends all He begins!

"For I know the plans I have for you," declares the LORD,
"plans to prosper you and not to harm you, to give you hope
and a future." (*Jeremiah 29:11,* NIV)

Joan Elbourn

In Or Out

To implode or to explode
                that's the question?

The option is quite simple . . .
                yet profound.

For one implies destruction
                      by suggestion;
          the other splatters pieces
                            all around.

Now some may wonder why such questions haunt me
        and if it really matters how one dies.

But I will have the answers to what taunts me . . .

     "Which way's she blow?"
          is more than Ahab's cry!

General contributor

Sticks And Stones

As a butterfly, as it flits . . . .

lights . . . . and then it's gone

Are the sweet sweet words of encouragement

I need to sing my song.

As a net, as it covers over . . . .

twists . . . . distorts. . . . defrays,

Are the shattering words of discouragement

I live with many a day.

Kay Kocour

The Death Of A Job

Happening on a summer's day —
A noise I'd known before —
It was the sound of death I heard,
And once again — *my* door.
    The letter came unexpectedly,
    Addressed in formal tones;
    In cold and plain hard terms it said,
    "Take all your effects; and go home."
Egads, I thought — this is a shock!
Why did this letter come?
Then I cried and mourned the loss,
While part of me stayed numb.
    It's taken a while to recuperate.
    The job was a big part of me.
    But now I know and can truly say
    I sense God's grace so free.
Offers have come and been turned down;
They're not the right job yet.
One of these days *that* job will come
And I won't have a regret.
    So beyond the veil of tears and cries
    I look to see God's plan.
    This may be one of those difficult times
    When it's "on the shelf" for Jan.
"On the shelf" isn't a terrible place
But it takes a bit of adjustment
When you're the one who's sitting there
And trying to figure a budget.
    I have to trust in God's keeping power;
    He has the plan for me.
    And when the time is totally right
    His plan for me I'll see.
At that point I can move on and go;
I won't have to feel like a blob.
Once more I'll know that I can live
And survive — the death of a job.

Jan Widman

Pain

The pain is so intense yet I feel numb. . .
        like a movie fan forgetting reality
            while watching old familiar films,
   stealing emotions from two-dimensional people
        alive only on a screen.

Where does this pain come from?
What chain reaction culminates in this dull ache
        within my bones
            and lust for death within my soul?

What purpose can it have —
        attacking me so unexpectedly
          amidst my everyday duties,
   leaving me paralyzed and lethargic
        feeling worthless and alone?

Why is there no secret healing
        to purge this deathly pain I bear?
   What price to cleanse this evil from within?
Do I have enough to pay the price?
        Can it be worth the cost?

Oh, pain deep in my soul, how were you born?
    How will you die?
    Will I die with you?
    Have I already?
    Are you all that's left . . .
        of the person God wanted me to be?

Patty Lane

Heart Sounds

A broken heart screams out in pain . . .

    pieces fall with a tragic sound

        of fallen rain . . . . to a sad refrain

settling to the ground.

These sounds are life . . . . even red with strife

    hymn sung on bended knee . . . .

        but who can bear a silent heart . . . .

Oh, Lord, how can this be?

Kay Kocour

Pride

Thoughts Along The Way

Do you suppose that God

    in His wisdom,

    knew that if He made me

    one bit more adequate,

I would never lean on Him?

Betty Reber

Victim

As I move through the muck and mire

of life, I cry out in aggravation!

My humanity screams, my countenance beams

with the anger of sin's retribution.

Perchance should I look to His promises true

to the heavens, home of His grace,

My prideful will is transformed in a trill

as I view true humility's face.

Yes, my troubles melt like a spring fallen snow

as my eyes behold I Am,

deflation as a loosed balloon . . .

are my frustrations in light of the Lamb.

Kay Kocour

The Potter's Hands

(Jeremiah 18:1–6)

As a vessel I am useless, Lord,
Unless I'm filled with You.
Though I strive with all my might
My self-willed efforts just won't do.

I've pulled away from the Potter's hands,
The work He started put on hold.
I'm chipped and marred, battered and worn
I refused to let His plan unfold.

The Potter's wheel sits silent; still,
His eager hands are poised above
Waiting for my submissive will
To yield to the molding of His love.

I want to turn back to the Potter,
Be that shapeless lump of clay,
And let His hands begin afresh
To form my life to walk His way.

Lord, take my bitter, lonely years;
Grind them into dust. Then blend it
Gently; mix it with your tender tears
And use that clay as you intended.

I yield now to the Potter's hands
Convinced of His consummate skill.
He made me, so He understands
Just how to mold me to His will.

There's joy in resting in those hands,
As I perceive His goal.
He'll spin the wheel, He'll smooth and shape
And I'll be completely mended, whole.

Lois Williams

Compromise

Letting Go

Rarely does a quiet mind come to visit

for being obsessive compulsive with its whirling "do's" have
taken up permanent residence.

Lord, may they realize their presence as only past protection
for which I am thankful.

But the time has come for them to pack up all their
"belongings"

  . . . . and to go.

Rita McIlwain

Compromise (Death and Dying)

Sometimes life takes you by surprise
Something hits you square between the eyes
Those are the times
It's hard to remember
Who's the fool
and who is wise.

Those are the times to turn inside
When the strongest urge is to run and hide
To shrink from life
To be safely invisible
O found-out child
No one can see you now.
                    if

. . . .
       success .
           .
          .   is not
. . . .
               attainable .
. . . .
    . then
     . .
       .
   attaining .
. . . .
. failure
. . . .
       becomes .
      .
     .   a kind of
. . . .
                   .
                   .
                   .
           success .
        . . . .

Monica C. Page

Homemade

Inside my heart a child exists,
              she knows so very much.
But I'm afraid to know her pain,
              so why reach out to touch?
Perhaps there's more than simple pain
              inside this one in me.
But until now that's all I've found,
              it's all there is to see.

It brings to mind my question
              about what gave her such pain
and how a child could be so scared
              that inside she'd remain.
I suppose it seemed a safe place,
              not much going on in there
for without the child set free in me,
              my heart can never care.

Will she ever know what scared her so
              and when the ache began
Or does our God have reasons
              to keep secrets in His plan?

Can we two live together . . .
              or is there room for only one?
I can't ignore her presence.
              By her strength I think she's won.

[continued]

The struggle grows between us
               and has gone too far to quit.
The little one controls my heart,
               but can't make me submit.

Please find a way that we can grow
               together unafraid?
For we are wounded children . . .
               that were thoroughly homemade!

General contributor

Aimlessness

Senseless

The pain explodes . . .
   yet I feel not a thing.

The memories flood . . .
   but no answers they bring.

Bold actions flash . . .
   yet there's nothing to see.

Loud sounds resound . . .
   but no noise reaches me.

While senses are silent
   within there's a cry . . .

It's faint and it's small
   and my heart wonders why.

Can there ever be peace in this life filled with pain?
   and where is the meaning
      when one feels insane?

General contributor

I Wonder

I don't want to think
I'm so tired of thinking.

I don't want to try
I'm so tired of trying.

Will I ever enjoy the freedom
to simply be?

What is it like to be?
I wonder . . .
    To be whole
    To be free
    To know who you are.
    To be comfortable with peace that
      abides inwardly and out.
    What is it like to be?
I wonder . . .
    To arise in the morning and greet the sun with a smile
    To have a clear mind that allows the wind and songs of
      birds to whisper mysteries
To laugh and feel. . . and even run
To breathe deep the air that fills your whole being with
    life
What is it like to be?

I wonder . . . . I wonder.

Rita McIlwain

being there
should not take
so much energy
being there
is effortless
why
is
it
so
hard
to be
here
there
anywhere
to
be
completely

Jolanta B. Uniejewski

not
knowing
where
it
is
going
to
lead
I
ask
uneasy
questions
say
some
painful
truths
and
describe
the
way
I
feel
about
you

I
say
I
don't
love
anymore
I
say
I
don't
care
anymore

[continued]

I
say
I
feel
empty
inside
and
"NO!"
sex
will
not
fix
it

and
"NO!"
time
will
not
heal
it

and
"YES!"
I
don't
know
what
to
do.

Jolanta B. Uniejewski

Ridicule

Fat . . . Ugly . . . Stupid

FAT. . . UGLY . . . STUPID.
Relentlessly the litany of self-hatred
hammers away at her battle-weary brain.

FAT . . . UGLY . . . STUPID.
Spawned by a single act of degradation so deep,
the hideous imprint stamped indelibly on her soul.

FAT. . . UGLY . . . STUPID.
Reinforced by "well-meaning" relatives
who justify themselves in picking away at
the fragile strands of a child's self-esteem
with prying questions and disapproving glances.

FAT . . . UGLY. . . STUPID.
Telephone that never rang. Dates that never happened.
Cruel remarks by thoughtless schoolmates
that replayed endlessly like broken records.

FAT . . . UGLY . . . STUPID.
Mirrors that jeered back in contempt.
Ill-fitting clothes.
Awkward silences for social graces never learned.

FAT . . . UGLY . . . STUPID.
Academic achievements, recognition from friends.
Pounds lost . . .
Still nothing can erase those well-worn tracks in her brain.

FAT . . . UGLY . . . STUPID.
The painful journey of healing is begun,
and the haunting, accusing voices
grow less frequent and emphatic.

FAT . . . UGLY . . . STUPID.
Learning to question the questions, to doubt the doubts.
Waging war against this insidious enemy
instead of lying down in defeat.

FAT . . . UGLY . . . STUPID.
Crying out to her Maker,
longing for a transforming word
from Him who speaks beauty into being.
Across the pages of time,
ageless words from a relentlessly loving Father
find their way to her aching, hungry heart . . .

". . . you will be called by a new name that the mouth of the LORD
will bestow. You will be a crown of splendor in the LORD's hand . .
. . No longer will they call you Deserted . . . . But you will be called
Hephzibah . . . for the LORD will take delight in you . . . . as a
bridegroom rejoices over his bride, so will your God rejoice over
you." *Isaiah 62:2b-5* (NIV)

FAT . . . UGLY . . . STUPID.
The words still come back to haunt,
but lose the power to harm
when confronted with the Living Word,
who patiently sows seeds of love and truth in the heart of
his bride.

Judy Johnson

Awakened by the phone
annoyed
and yet half dreaming
I hear the piercing voice
from far
commanding operator
to make it work
mother
and then
the change
softness
concern
care
but the other tone
is still in the air

why don't we write
what's new
she wonders, worries
she will explain later
what am I doing wrong
but
she has changed
is not the same
she understands
nevertheless
I should not dig into my childhood
it wasn't all that bad
and I should respect

I say
I'll write
and gathering courage
I tell her
I couldn't before
cause I disagreed with her

my pain is back
it returned the same second
she mentioned the past

Jolanta B. Uniejewski

Rejection

You Couldn't Hear

I thought you'd stay . . .
   It came with words like
     "I love you"
     and
     "Till death do us part."

You spoke with integrity of the term
     commitment
It seemed to be worked
   into the very fiber
     of your being.

But . . .

That was before you left,
before you said,
     "I can't handle what you're going through,"

before I hurt, felt helpless
  and let myself need you.

"I don't like neediness," you said.
          I told you it would pass;

            you couldn't hear.

General contributor

Riddle Me This . . .

I see you thru a long black tunnel now.

        The distance
                at one moment
                        minimizes who you were . . .
     at another .

          .
           .

                maximizes the distortion.

What we once were
        fades into shadows of obscurity.

Could it be that I've never really known you,
                touched you,
                      experienced you?

Are you little more than a clearinghouse . . .
                of endless duty
                    and grinding responsibility;

       trapped and imprisoned
                    by the guilt of poor choices
                       or feared failure. . .
                  suffocated by even the thought
                    of human intimacy?

The distance between us is growing:
                we are not.

     Can nothing shrink such gaping voids?

For in this world of riddles

    where all things face destruction,

        why can't enemies like

            .

                distance

                    .

                     .

                    be destroyed?

                General contributor

I Cried

Sometimes I just can't face
What he does to me.
How she hurts me.
I go into a corner and cry until I feel
Something inside me.

Just give me a push,
An encouraging word or two
Then I know I can face
What he does to me.
How she hurts me.

Who picks me up when I'm down
Who brushes away my tears
Who says "Hello," when no one else does.
Who shows me the way when no one's around.

God will be my friend,
Win or lose, to the end
He'll even cry with me.

Jana Ruth Holiday
(Age 11)

There's No Such Thing

There are broken hearts,
broken promises and dreams;
irreconcilable differences, loneliness,
and maybe a touch of remorse.
But think it through and you will find,
there's no such thing as divorce.

There are stepchildren,
ex-wives, second chances,
restraining orders, personal property,
the dog, the cat, the Porsche;
but if truth ever finds reality,
there's no such thing as divorce.

There are depositions, counselors,
alimony, attorney's fees
that would choke a horse;
but bottom line my friend,
there's no such thing as divorce.

Kay Kocour

Of Questionable Value

I've become like a piece of furniture to you, my dear,
        a semipriceless antique . . .
                of questionable value.

You sit me in a corner now
        "out of the way," you say,

        in the shadows . . .
                unnoticed . . .

        less likely to be an obstacle
                to automated progress.

It must be a relief to you
                putting things in such order,

        simplifying the issues and demands
                that take up precious time and resources,

        leaving you free to obsess in isolation and silence.

Everything is set aside now,
        making it easier for you
                to focus on pursuit of the dream.

Midlife engraves its crisis
                in the furrows of your brow.

No less than making the team will please you,
                a team made up of winners . . .
                        purveyors of great gain.

And then at last
        you'll finally know success—
                that peculiar changing state—
                        so flagrantly undefinable.

But what if that ideal escapes your grasp?
        Will life be worth the grief of shattered goals . . .
                or will you then decide to rid your plans
                        of antique furniture . . .
                                and journey on?

General contributor

Rejection Reflection

REJECT — unwilling to accept, recognize,
or make use of; repudiate, deny; throw out,
discard; throw back, spurn, dismiss.

Rejection is real. It happens every day. Say hello to
someone and they may refuse to recognize your greeting. Take
mail from the mail box, before you're inside, three or four
pieces hit the garbage can unopened and unread. Stop to pick
up a few things at the market, squeeze the lemons, and the
hard ones are replaced on the stand aren't they? Someone
offers you a sample and you walk right past mumbling
something like "I've already eaten." On the way home, a
hitchhiker thumbs at you and you thumb him back.

There are worse types of rejection — getting fired from a
job. Reasons here are important. It could be your fault (a
shoddy performance) but there could be other reasons.

The husband says he's in love with another woman — tells you
not to take it personally when he leaves. He's either stupid
or insane or both. That's a type of rejection — it's called
murder.

There is one type even worse — child abuse in its different
forms, emotional, physical and mental. The perpetrator
executes, then at some point in time rejects . . . the last fiber
that was that child is broken. That's not rejection, that's
an abomination. The future of that child is bleak for any of
the above discussed rejections can send her spiraling down
into the diabolical depths she once experienced and has tried
so hard to escape.

"My child, stay close to me. You can not escape rejection
but seek those experiences that will cause healthy growth."

Kay Kocour

More Boundaries

Like a thief
you broke into my heart
and like a thief
you left it empty.

It won't happen again
for I have learned
I can open, close or lock
my heart's door.

Kay Kocour

Unbelief

The Incested Damned

Sheol, our refuge, land of the living dead,
Where even if we hide, God's hand is there,
Yet, blind to His comfort we cringe from Him in dread,
And feel ourselves outcast with none to care.

And if God's hand should touch us though we cringe,
And we should feel our image in His palm,
Still we rest not in that place He has carved,
Our deep-shamed spirit writhes and is not calm.

Our torment twists, distorts our face and form,
The mold He carved for us feels like a grave,
No love can reach us and we must move on,
There is a child we still must try to save.

And God Himself can only watch in grief
As terror-filled His nomad children roam,
Never knowing comfort or relief
Homeless though we stand before our home.

Like parents of stolen children God pursues,
Following, though often far behind,
Perhaps before us, leading, we know not,
We are not only lost — to God we're blind.

His scattered flock are we, the ones incested,
We do not gather 'round Him with the herd,
The constant inner voice that we have used,
To block our memories, bars the Shepherd's words,

We never lie down long in pastures green,
His rod and staff don't lead us to our goal,
We wander back and forth eternally,
As comfortless in Heaven as in Sheol.

"Whither shall I go from thy Spirit? Or whither shall I flee from thy presence? If I ascend to heaven thou art there! If I make my bed in Sheol (the place of the dead), thou art there." *(Psalm 139:7–8*, RSV)

"See. I will not forget you. I have carved you on the palm of my hand." *(Isaiah 49:16*, RSV)

Janice Gail Knowlton

For Linnea

We wonder who the God is
Who stood on the sidelines
Watching as we were abused.

We, the children of God
Used, tortured and brutalized
By the parents we thought were Gods.

Did our heavenly Father suffer
Weeping with us as we died
Little by little, piece by piece?

Curling up small, stealing out of our minds
Out of our bodies,
leaving an empty shell
For our tormentors to enjoy?

And if God wept impotently
Unable to stand between us and evil
How can we now surrender all
Into his keeping?
Saying, THY will, not mine be done?

How can we again pray the unanswered prayer
Reaching out again in perfect trust
Reenter our minds, inhabit our bodies
Remove the armor of amnesia?

How can we creep into the lap of God
Curl peacefully against his breast
Gaze innocently into his eyes
Be vulnerable in his embrace
Have perfect trust in his care?

Yet we do trust again
Timidly and painfully we search
Among the haunting memories of the past
The unremembered ghosts we've hidden from.
Holding hands with other children
Whose lives, like ours, hide grief.

We tiptoe back in time
Shed our armor
Bear the pain of confrontation
With the captors of our lives.

Holding hands with other children
We talk alone, yet together
Into a future we can now create
Nurturing ourselves,
Parents to our inner child.

If there is a God as courageous as we,

He is welcome in our lives.

Janice Gail Knowlton

How Can I Trust?

How can I trust in a
God that allows
atrocities to happen . . . to me?

How can I believe in a
God that does not
protect children from wickedness?

Or did you . . . .

As the very psychological system
they so deftly
so wickedly
created
now turns to resist and advance,

Heaven cheers,

Jesus smiles

And I'm proud of what He has made of me.

Kay Kocour

Impatience

Why Am I Me?

I seek and I wander
I try and I roam
And I know there's an answer somewhere.
But searching the road
Burdened by loads,
Confusion can lead to despair.

So why should I rise?
And why should I sleep?
And why should I speak when they call?
And why should I search?
And why should I pray?
And why should I watch my dreams — fall?

I am weary and tired.
I am troubled and worn.
Loneliness fills every vein.
As I look around,
Answers others have found,
But why then . . .
Why am I, still me?

Rita McIlwain

Wait

Lord, You tell me to wait, but I am impatient.

Time is too precious to spend waiting.

You tell me You have a plan for my life,

but I am desperate and confused.

You lead me one way, and I feel that is the direction

You want me to follow.

When that direction becomes narrow, I feel frustrated

and bound by insecurity.

Lord, teach me to be patient and to wait.

For I know that they that wait on the Lord

shall renew their strength.

They will mount up with wings as eagles.

They will run and not get weary,

they will walk and not faint.

That's Your promise to us when we wait.

Marcee Ekstrum

Carrot-Stick God

I serve a carrot-stick God,
And I'm not at all awed,
By His tactical evasions
and maneuvers.

He offers me a clue
and to give Him His due
He opens a few
doors (mainly louvers).

I see part of the plan
I begin to think I can
unravel the mystery
resolve it.

Then my theory breaks down
I feel like a clown
I begin to believe
I'll never solve it.

But my carrot-stick God
offers another rod
and reels me in again
with the bait.

I rush ahead of Him
then things get grim
till I hear Him calling
"Please wait!"

Janice Gail Knowlton

Are We There Yet Daddy?

How come if you're my shepherd, I want?

Why is it I forage in pastures
of wilted high grasses
seeking and searching yet not satisfied?

How come if you're my shepherd, I want?

My path is choked with barbed remembrances
rocky and steep with jagged projections.

I pass streams that are raging with a savage resolve
drink from polluted pools with mocking reflections.

I AM HUNGRY.
I AM THIRSTY.
I AM WEARY.
I AM LONELY.

Truth is an abiding light . . . .
but goodness and mercy are nowhere in sight.

How come if you're my shepherd, I want?

Kay Kocour

Lord, Can You Hurry It Up?

Why does it hurt so much?

Lord, can You hurry it up?

Must I go through the valley so deep to

Get to the mountains? I chose this journey

Of healing, but can you hurry it up?

Can you see me Lord? Don't you know

What I'm going through? I see ashes, You

See beauty. I see weakness, You see strength.

I see despair, You are hope. Hold my hand

Lord, don't you let go. Hold my hand Lord,

Hold it tight, for my journey has begun.

Cindy Delsid

Hopelessness

Casualties

Within the weary walls of human luggage
                called the soul,
    There lies an instrument of war
                a hand-grenade grown old.

It makes its cold steel presence known
                with every breath I take . . .
    through frantic feelings, frenzied thoughts
                and words that hesitate.

'Twould seem like such a simple thing
                to just pull out the pin,
    and wait for flying fragments
                of the needy child within.

But this is not the world's to see . . .
                this private form of war
    though healthy ones may want to know
                how pain could reach so far.

For who is really enemy when weapons live inside?
    And why do we so foolishly call "losers" those who die?

Lana Bateman

No Way Out

The bomb within my chest longs to explode

The pain of its mere presence

contaminates my thoughts,

seducing me with claims of

"No way out . . . ."

An unknown panic now invades my mind

Releasing frenzy and its will to die

draining energies and firm resolve

thru sudden frantic screams of

"No way out . . . ."

The loneliness of what once was a home —

casts empty shadows on life's future dreams

While even weary councils of the night

all whisper in the darkness . . .

"No way out . . . ."

General contributor

Are You The One?

I am in pain; don't you care?
I am in prison; are you there?

Like John the Baptist of old, I am asking,
    "Are you the one who was to come or should I expect
        another?"

Your response remains the same.
You speak of your kingdom
    where
        the rejected are received;
        the dead have life;
        and the good news is preached.

Can't you hear my cries,
    "It is not fair;
        it is not right!
    Is this really love?
    Do you really care?"

Or am I, like John, simply waiting for the wrong answer?

Ruth McMath

Mistrust

Without Solution

When will I ever know small joys again?

    The symphony of spring
        with colors and textures exploding into view,

      the silky feel of babies' skin,

        sensations of a cool breeze blowing thru my hair.

They're all so far away now . . .
    the simple things
        that once filled my heart
          with awe for the God who made them.

In this peculiar place to which You've brought me . . .
        surroundings never change.

The seasons fill with faded browns and grays.

      Winter no longer takes with it . . .
          its bleak and dreary pall.

     and the soul's palette has limited hues
        with which to paint the fossils of its pain.

What seems to others . . . vibrant activity
      in picture filled with color
        is no more than a negative to me . . .

           processing incomplete.

Ghostly strips hung in developers' labs,
        each scene locked in space and time.
                                      .

                           .

                                  waiting.
Waiting for chemicals to induce glossy sheets
                filled with brilliant shades of life.

But what if no one comes to move these stark transparencies
        to magical solutions that transcend?

And what if these strange darkened strips
                should ever stay the same,
                      reflecting death immobilized within?

Then we condemned to lead these helpless lives
              would stay forever frozen in each frame . . .

And answers to such questions
              as,
                 "How shall we then know joy?"

        Could be withheld through Someone Else's whim.

                          General contributor

HOW
CAN
A THREE
YEAR
OLD
SAY
"I DON'T
WANT TO
PLAY
WITH
DOLLS
ANYMORE"
AND
GIVE
THEM
AWAY?

HOW
CAN
A CHILD
NEVER
SMILE
AND
HAVE
THAT
INTENSE
LOOK
ON THE FACE?

HOW
CAN
A
MOTHER

TELL
HER
ELEVEN-
YEAR-
OLD
DAUGHTER
THAT
SHE
JUST
HAD
AN ABORTION?

HOW
CAN I
NOW
AT
THIRTY
MAKE
THE
THREE
&
ELEVEN
YEAR
OLD
FEEL
SAFE
&
SECURE?

Jolanta B. Uniejewski

Trust

Trust is a mystery or maybe it's a trick
No one tells the children that without it you'll be sick.

I guess one assumes that it comes while she grows
But what of the child whose home's filled with foes?

Could there be a chance she could ever know how
To reach out in love and to live in the now?

If trust isn't transferred from those who provide
How can such a loss be recaptured inside?

Can she now become what God wants her to be
When the basis of growth is a heart that's set free?

How can she know freedom while always on guard?
And how does she heal the heart her own trust scarred?

Can she now learn trust or is it too late
To chip away walls that are sealing her fate?

The decision is hers, but her pain may not see
How to start life anew — learn to trust and be free!

Patty Lane

Hands That Touch

I've wondered for a while about a theory I assert.
    It seems to me to be the truth . . .
        all hands that touch must hurt.

I can't remember when I first began to know this fact
    but when bad things would happen . . .
        my mind would just react.

God gave us hands for reasons, not making them inert.
    but surely He did not intend . . .
        to give us hands to hurt.

All hands just look the same to me, four fingers and a thumb.
    But someone's hands once trusted,
        left my heart and body numb.

So now it helps to know the rule — "With all hands be alert."
    No longer stupid — I found truth
        that all hands make me hurt.

It's true enough, it took my joy and left me only pain.
    Where cruelty of life goes on . . .
        Can God and love remain?

Then one day taken by surprise, new hands reached out to care
    but can I, after all these years
        find trusting hands to share?

I wasn't sure until I felt my own hands soiled with dirt.
    Then silently those gentle hands
        cleansed mine without a hurt.

Those tender hands brought healing and a growing hope within
    that one day I might learn to say,
        "I trust in hands again."

Patty Lane

Temporary Relief

Gardening

Never use the weed-eater

on the crabgrass of your soul.

You have to DIG that out!

Betty Reber

a lot of anesthetic
beer
wine
cigarettes
the pain
so unbearable . . .
you are
afraid
of making statements
with
your works
like
Andy Warhol
who said
"nothing"
when
asked
what
does
his
picture
mean

Jolanta B. Uniejewski

Self-Pity

Lazarus Disturbed

Sometimes,
    I just feel sorry for myself
        hoping someone . . . somewhere
            will call or come.
Truthfully, I don't know if I care
        to hear another voice
            or see a face.

No,
    It's not easy to escape
        this world
            or find a quiet place
                to numb your mind . . .
to let the time go by
        without a sound
            with no one there to please . . .
                no frenzied pace.

So,
    Where can I now go
        to find such peace . . .
            a place where loneliness
                is called a friend
And no one calls me forth from Lazarus's tomb
        and beckons me . . .
            return to life again?

Lana Bateman

It's Party Time

Self-pity is not much of a party . . . .

    invite some friends and see

        empty places in echoing spaces

myself as company.

There is One who is always there

    when into myself I try to hide.

        Comes to me, draws me out you see.

shows me His hands and His feet and His side.

Kay Kocour

Unworthiness

If

If I can only find myself in the light of your eyes
and in your approval — I am forever lost.

If I can only see my worth mirrored from your face
and hear it in your voice — I am forever blind and deaf.

If all you did to me . . . or refused to do
defines my ability to live and love today,
then I am only a reflection of you — and not myself at
all.

Lana Bateman

Marginal People (in between two worlds)

I always felt
like there
was a flaw
in me
as if I was
born different
and never
was one of them —
couldn't belong

For many years
I tried to adapt
and was successful
to some degree
but
much of what I said
I said
out of hurt,
pain and defensiveness

I knew, though
that there must be
a place for people
like me
and I found this place
it's a CONEY ISLAND
OF THE MIND

Jolanta B. Uniejewski

My Knight Who Rides Alone

If there was ever a knight in shining armor . . . it was Jeff.
He has always been the oak that I could lean on
to find shelter in the storms life brought my way.

How easy to take him for granted
. . . always coming home
. . . always being faithful
. . . always showing me nothing but love.

I guess I have been a very hard person to live with —
anything but normal.
What is normal?

I am afraid my knight wants to come down off his horse and
walk away
. . . What would this damsel in distress do?
. . . How could I blame one who has fought off my dragons
for so long?

But I grieve tonight
My heart aches deep within and my mind taunts me with
thoughts I never entertain.
I am in my lonely tower.

My knight is here somewhere
But I know not exactly where . . .
. . . He is roaming and keeping all his secrets to himself
. . . Maybe he isn't sure what all the secrets even are
. . . He has hidden them deep in his armor . . .
Where no one can get at them.

I am a damsel with no hair
My breast is gone and only scars remain
My body is tired and weak.
My mind and emotions are in battle against me . . .
I have nothing to offer.

Should I expect anyone to remain in all of this?
I am no prize to cherish . . .
Only extra baggage to a knight who rides alone.

I fear he wants to shed his knightly image
. . . . . and be free.

I understand — my beloved knight — for bondage has been
my life.

Rita McIlwain

Recycled For The Lord

Today I feel like . . .
    A used firecracker or a balloon with a hole
    in it. An outdated dress. A dried-up pen.
    An empty pop can. A worn-out shoe. A
    discarded blob of bubble gum. Yesterday's crumpled newspaper.

. . . Sometimes I feel so worthless, Lord,
    And it seems I can't do anything right.
    Just close my mouth at those times
    When I need to listen.
    Help me talk when I hold everything
    Inside.

Refill this empty shell with
    Your Presence, Lord.
    Remind me that I'm special —
    If only because when You died
    On the Cross —
    You did it for me.

Recycle me into something
    That will be used for Your glory
    As You pick up my body (NO DEPOSIT) . . .
    Which has been discarded (NO RETURN),
    Along the highway of life . . .

Jo Winkowitsch

Fear

Wholly Yours

Lord, I peel back my "cover"

    and totally expose my heart.

Even I cannot discern all that it holds.

So come. . . .

    examine this heart of mine.

As I hold the moving covers

    my hands may shake . . .

My eyes may flinch in uncertainty

but come, MY LORD, examine . . .

    and make this heart . . .

    wholly yours.

Rita McIlwain

Servant Of A Lesser God

Palpitation . . . . incarnation,

fear that paralyzes

denies a power greater than itself

and spurs the mind's flight into cowardice.

Past pathos triggered by present passions

need not affect today

for intimidators, exterminators

are alive only in my memory's eye.

Listen to its rhythm

what it's saying is a lie . . . refute the lie

and like a loosed balloon its potency vanishes

swallowed by a deep blue sky.

Its earthbound agent is now powerless,

see him as he really is and choose to live in love.

Pity him, for he has not yet escaped like you

and remains a servant of a lesser god.

Kay Kocour

Be Still

Be still and know that I am God;

Still your heart of every call.

Rein your thoughts of random wandering,

In quietness on your knees fall.

Be still and find I am a refuge,

Though waters roar and mountains quake,

Though your life be full of tumult,

Know I will never move or shake.

Be still and in this quiet find

From me flows a calm, a strength,

For I'm always in control,

Will be exalted yet, at length.

Be still, be still; in the stillness

My ever present help is near.

Of all that life could ever bring you,

Still know I'm God and do not fear.

"Be still, and know that I am God." (*Psalm 46:10*, KJV)

Edith Martin

Afraid

I stare at this page, afraid.

My heart pounds and with each pulse I am drawn deeper into my own soul and into my own deep pain.

Disintegrating, slowly and painfully, is the glue that has held my life together. With its disappearance comes an ache so powerful it overwhelms the tiny fragments of my heart that so tenuously lie together on the floor of my soul.

I have longed to be free from the glue that discolors and disfigures my heart.

But the force pulling it from the crevices reveals yet still uglier scars from years gone by. The rawness it leaves behind and the sensitivity it once covered and protected is now exposed and hurting.

I beg for the familiar glue to return but instead I know that this time my heart must be shaped in the symmetry that God intended. No glue or crack filler, but rather small broken pieces, cracked and bruised, lovingly smoothed and polished to be uniquely mine.

Patty Lane

All through the dark, quiet night,
with just the soft glow of the clock light
I pray, watch, and wait,
for the wet tears, not sure how to release the gate
and all the fears and nightmares,
that haunt such a small boy.
Brush the hair from your forehead,
not sure what words should be left unsaid.
Such long lashes and sad, brown eyes,
making me want to hold you and hum a lullaby;
and stop your small, trembling shoulders,
not wanting your heart to turn any colder.
Such a little boy,
to have to contend with new fears.
But I am here and will always be near,
through all the long night
even though I can't make everything all right.
Wish I could erase any bad memories,
so I'll do whatever is necessary
to help ease the hard lesson that's being taught,
and avoid getting tangled up in the web and
    forever caught,
leaving scars that hopefully won't be too deep.
Oh, please find a peaceful sleep,
dream of playmates, ice pops, and silly games,
even though our life is not the same.
The hour is past midnight, so late,
but I'll spend the long night with you and wait,
and hold you, wiping your tears,
letting you know how much I care;
As I hold you with closed eyes, I whisper my prayers.

Christine Reinecke

Learning To Trust

God . . . . .

I'm so frightened, scared;

So scared.

Please don't touch me.

I'm so afraid,

That somehow,

I might get hurt,

Again.

After so very many disappointments,

I am learning to trust,

In things unseen.

I think that's called Faith.

I'm scared of someone else

Knowing all my secrets,

And turning away.

But I'm even more afraid,

That I will be left behind,

Because I couldn't trust.

Elizabeth Arakelian

Isolation / Loneliness

The Little Glazed Sculpture

Winter came early and would not depart
Winter came early to a tender young heart.

Frozen inside, the child would not feel.
Locked in her pain she could not heal.

Icy responses replaced her trust.
Numbed by life's season
                her soul formed a crust.

Hardened by bitterness,
                chilled with despair.
Encased in the cold with no one to care.

Icicle tears clung to her face,
Frigid reminders of her shame and disgrace.

Winter came early to a tender young heart,
Winter came early and would not depart.

Spring finally came late in her years,
Spring finally came to thaw her tears.

The little glazed sculpture
                stood frozen in place,
Till the light of the Son
                dissolved her disgrace.

The icicles fell to the ground below,
Her heart warmed with love
                melted the snow.

No longer a statue in an ice-cold rhyme,
No longer a victim locked in a crime.

Spring finally came to thaw her tears,
Spring finally came late in her years.

Patsy Clairmont

The Winter Of My Mind

Winter, cold, gray, lonely.
Thank God it somehow passes into spring.

Just as the darkest night gives way to day,
The great reliever,

When all your sad and lonely thoughts shall pass,
Will slip away

As does the winter frost
When spring at last bursts forth
to soothe the dampened soul.

For some, there are no springs, no quiet dawns.
I can't remember feeling light or free.

I've lived a thousand winters in this cave,
The soul's own prison, locked.
There is no key.

Do I seem to stare beyond you when you speak?
I seldom hear your words.

It's not that I don't want to share your springs,
But while you speak

An icy wind comes drifting through my mind.
I've closed the door.

I build my fires alone.

Lana Bateman

Where Do You Go?

It's hard for me to stay right here
                I've never known just why it's so.
But for some time I've wondered why
                My body stays while my mind goes.

It flies to my own secret place
                far from people I have known.
When I can't bear the pain or hurt
                where I feel safe is where I've gone.

I've often wanted just to live there
                although I'd be all alone.
It gives me peace, turns out the lights
                and keeps my secrets still unknown.

General contributor

being there
should not take
so much energy
being there
is effortless
why
is
it
so
hard
to be
here
there
anywhere
to
be
completely

Jolanta B. Uniejewski

With the light filtering in from underneath the door,
she sits crouched under the covers,
    holding back the tears,
knowing only that she expected more
than the usual nondescript stare.
Clutching her doll, so tightly in her hand,
    that she's caught
listening apprehensively for the expected shouts
that don't appear to intrude tonight upon her thoughts,
leaving her with her usual fears and doubts.
But tonight, enveloped in the silence
is a sadness and a fear of being alone,
that all of her small body is so tense,
she almost lets out a moan.
She blinks back the tears,
remembering the scene that took place before.
All she wanted was recognition and maybe a dear,
but failing again as his daughter once more.
Always striving for perfection,
without slamming the door,
while left wondering if she'll ever
    head in the right direction.
So again left standing on the outside,
looking in at distorted figures,
not knowing if she should run and hide
or how much more she can endure.
Seeking comfort, she turns to her side,
her hand reaches up, tracing the cross, that's hers,
as it hangs on her wall, day and night.
So with these thoughts floating thru her mind,
sleep finally arrives with eyes shut tight,
with hope that tomorrow the world will be kind,
to a little girl who is too tired to fight
and cope any longer with another sleepless night.

Christine Reinecke

I'll Think Of The Good Memories

I'll think of the ranch, of good memories so I won't
bash my head on the tile in the kitchen breaking my thick
skull bones till it bursts like a ripe tomato.

I'll think of my favorite memory — riding horses, the
smell of hay on them, the sound of the hot leather straps
rubbing against each other, the feel of the short coarse
horse hair, and the long wiry mane that I hold onto when I'm
riding bareback. The sound of the shoed horses as they clip
clop softly in the powdery chestnut color dirt.
So I won't get up and go into the kitchen for a long,
sharp knife to stop my heart from beating.

I let my mind wander to the fruit trees in the orchard —
peaches, pears, green apples, plums, to pretend that I
am hungry and God hand feeds me because He loves me so much.
The plums are my favorite. The taut skin's a little tart and
the inside so sweet.

I won't let myself think about a gun, any gun, and how
good it would feel up against my temple, cold and hard and
only a finger pull away from this hell.

I loved the way my dad would cook up as many silver
dollar pancakes as we could eat — on a wood burning stove and
we would have a contest to see who could eat the most.

I think the best way would be a car accident off a
winding mountain road, put my foot to the floor and fly
through the air into sweet nothingness.

Or, God, if you would just tuck me in bed tonight and
please, please let me sleep forever.

General contributor

Rainbows

Rainbows are pretty.

Rainbows are sweet.

Rainbows are flying right down the street.

> When you're here I don't need you,
> but when I need you, you're not here!
> You are so beautiful I hate to see you go!

Rainbow rainbow rainbow!

Megan Chisom
(Megan is a seven year old
who wrote this during
the divorce of her parents.)

Chain Link Walls

I remember chain link walls —
the tears running down my cheek;
the other boys are playing ball
at school down by the creek.

They asked me in to play
but all you said was "no"
A part of me died that day —
you never seemed to know.

I wanted so to play
there on the other side.
You never saw my heart that day —
you never knew I cried.

It was only half a block
to school where they stayed
But I knew then you'd never walk
that far to see me play.

I remember chain link walls —
my fingers laced tightly through
I only wanted to go play ball,
but more, I wanted you.

I remember chain link walls —
the tears running down my cheek;
The other boys still play ball
at school down by the creek.

Bill Irwin

The loneliness within my life
　　　is more than I can bear
It's unacceptable to me
　　　but yet my Savior cares.
For he knew loneliness
　　　as we will never know,
when on the cross for me He died,
　　　His love the world to show.

The emptiness within my heart
　　　the grief alone I've kept,
but Jesus knows, for it was there
　　　at Lazarus's tomb He wept.
I must commit my sorrow to Him
　　　only He can bear the load.
The cross He carried was heavy that day
　　　as He walked up death's dark road.

He was so willing to die for me
　　　the least that I can do,
is glory in my hardships
　　　and know He'll see me through.
Then I'll look back upon my life
　　　and know He held my hand,
through trial upon trial
　　　now passed in Heaven's land,
where no loneliness, emptiness, sorrow are known
　　　just happiness, joy, and peace;
the harvest of earth's trials grown
　　　transformed by His sweet release.

Jean S. Christianson

On Being Alone

It has often occurred to me

that the church's

vision of me is blurred.

I come week by week, all year through,

not only to minister,

but to be ministered to.

Often I leave with the feeling

that no one understands the loneliness

that I am sometimes concealing.

Now I know how Jesus felt

when surrounded by the loneliness

of Calvary's cross

and the sins of the world

were thrust upon Him.

I can understand the despair of His words,

"My God, my God, why has thou forsaken me?"

For He was utterly alone.

I can treasure His gift as my own

for I could never be as lonely

as He was then.

Where men will fail me, Jesus does not.

Where others may leave me, Jesus will not.

He has promised,

"I will never leave thee nor forsake thee."

I am never completely alone

for He is always there.

Joseph L. Hamel

five
REWARDS

Rewards will come when we travel toward wholeness in Him! When we realize that we were created to trust Him, to love Him, and to worship and serve Him above all things, we become increasingly aware of God's call and purpose in our lives. Indeed, removing the blinders of emotional dysfunction helps to open hearts and senses to God's further revelation of Himself.

The human spirit has a great yearning for *purpose*. The first step toward the fulfillment of this longing is the person, Jesus Christ. Not until that need is met will the seeker come to peace with self and others. Once we know Christ as Savior and Lover of our souls, we desire to find our place and purpose in His kingdom.

A *renewed vitality* begins to emerge as we come to a place of greater healing. One young woman described feeling like a colt set loose to run free in the meadow. Another explained renewed vitality as climbing to higher ground with beautiful new vistas. She said that, in spite of the pain, she could never turn back. She described that new higher ground as a place where you breathe more freely and see Christ Jesus in ways you have never dreamed.

If the only assurance we were ever given in recovery were that of more *intimacy* with *Jesus, others,* and *ourselves,* it would still be worth the journey. What a glorious hope we have to draw nearer to the heart of God! In spite of all the pain, anger, and struggles along the way, these poems express a desire to be one with God. Before we can adequately love others, however, we must be able to see ourselves as loved, accepted, and cherished by God.

The road to intimacy is not an easy one. Few choose to take that step from personal isolation to genuine vulnerability. Those who do will continue to move toward spiritual and emotional growth on the road to recovery.

God ultimately draws us to a new *peace*. This peace does not exclude the realities of life, but accepts and functions within the difficulties of our own personal experience. As we see God working in our lives, we develop the peace and confidence to grasp the heavenly perspective of our earthly circumstances.

When we think of *heaven*, our tendency is to think only of that distant place and time when we will see Jesus face to face. While heaven is our eternal home with Him, a part of the kingdom is right here on earth. Remember, Jesus said, ". . . behold, the kingdom of God is within you" (*Luke 17:21*, KJV). We are not limited to heaven only as a future hope, but can live and love His kingdom through our healing hearts in the here and now.

Perhaps you are a seasoned traveler on the healing journey who has begun to experience some of the rewards described in these poems. We rejoice with you. However, even if you are in the early stages of recovery, the poetry shared here will encourage your soul in the days ahead.

If you are new to the concept of a journey to wholeness, these poems may stir in you the beginning of new healing. They may arouse a desire in you to minister to wounded hearts. Whatever your response, we pray that you will not close this book and remember only the abuse so many have suffered. Our prayer instead is that you will observe with righteous indignation what humans are capable of perpetrating against each other and then look beyond to all that God can bring forth from the ashes of destruction.

Robert Louis Stevenson said it well:

"When I first saw the terrible devastations of leprosy in Hawaii, I was almost turned into an infidel. But when I saw the miracle of Christian pity and compassion in the leper hospital at Molokai, my faith emerged triumphant, and I wrote in the guest book there:

> To see the infinite pity of this place,
> The mangled limb, the devastated face.
> The innocent sufferer smiling at the rod —
> A fool was tempted to deny his God.
>
> He sees, he shrinks. But if he gaze again.
> Lo, beauty springing from the breast of pain!
> He marks the cisterns on the mournful shores;
> And even a fool is silent and adores."

Purpose

Broken Things

It is an amazing thing
    awesome wondrous thing
        who and what the Lord uses . . . .
           broken things
           twisted things
           useless hopeless things
           foolish things.
I take heart in attic things
for if I am none of these, I need not a savior.
    Therefore, I will be thankful in my
        brokenness
        twistedness
        useless hopelessness
        foolishness.
    When I am weak, I am strong,
for He is making me whole, useful, hopeful and wise.

Kay Kocour

A Woman

A woman can learn,
   a woman can dream.
She can crochet
   or turn up a seam.
Her hands are gentle,
   her eyes are bright.
She has tender concern
   for a child in the night.
A woman is soft
   in a pretty dress,
or fights if she must —
   under great stress.
She's like a pathfinder,
   seeking new ways
to grow and to blossom.
   With each new day
she manages home,
   children, career.
Yet she still finds time
   to calm every fear.
She sees the treasure
   that life can bring,
being a woman's
   a marvelous thing.
The Lord gave woman
   a special place,
for she was inspired
   by His infinite grace.

Eve Bailey

The Message Of The Leaves

They all start green,

Then turn

To reds, yellows, browns —

More giving, more beautiful now.

Colleen Cooper

Renewed Vitality

April 1991

Thanks for April, Father
Flowers new-budded opening their petals
In simple worship
The wind, caressing softly the damp
Warming ground
And the ocean, Lord
Like diamonds, it dances

Birds' songs once more fill the air
Twittering in the early morning
Even flies, bees once more
Flitter and buzz
These, too, dance

And I, Lord?
I can't help feel new
Anticipating spring —
Like your creatures
I find myself in awe of you —
Creator, Yahweh
And because of all you do
All you are

I too dance

Joan Elbourn

Lord, There Are DAYS!

There are days I long to withdraw,
Safe within this shell that's me.
I must learn to look around "me."
For there are people . . . lost and hurting . . .
Who ask for someone to share their burdens.
I must not be afraid to care.
There are certainly circumstances
That could cripple me
If I don't look past them.
I must see good in everything.
There are decisions that confuse me
As I struggle to control my life.
I must see good in everything.
There are prayers waiting to be uttered.
Believing, trusting, petitioning, praising.
I must anchor my life in prayer.
Then there is the peace God freely offers
Causing the days, people, circumstances,
Decisions and prayers to
Make sense of my life.
I must learn to appreciate them.
And, in doing so,
I will finally be fulfilled,
As I venture out from within.

Jo Winkowitsch

Who Strikes The Blow?

I'm a victim of the year
When the warrior watched with fear
And the mighty one today
Trembled weakly, scared to play
And replacing tender touch
There was vile, untrusted lust —
Who strikes the blow?

From their rage, my sure demise
Hidden pain behind those eyes
Words of comfort go unheard
No one speaks forbidden words
Of the lie within the walls
And the screams that fill the halls —
Who strikes the blow?

And as childhood hatred grows
They seek today to gain control
Of another, small and weak
Looking up from disturbed sleep
Wishing only to escape
Another's pain and their dark place —
Who strikes the blow?

Looking back to pain's dark cage
Many victims cry in rage
From within the sickness grows
All it touches lose control
And a death resides inside
Guilt cries out through hopeless eyes —
Who strikes the blow?

[continued]

But in the healing of a prayer
Now a Savior I see there
Reaching gently to caress
All who rock in emptiness
And I look from different view
At that monster I once knew —
He stopped the blows!

Now such tiny hands I hold
And with wonder I behold
Bouncing, twirling, happy, free
Was this treasure born of me?
Oh, the sweetness waiting there
In the healing of the prayer —
He stopped the blows!

Patti Trimm

Easter

A brand new life, a growing love, power to be what
    you've called from above.
Tiny green leaves, lavender flowers
    all of creation — impassioned power.
Indeed you are the romantic ones, creators
Father, Spirit and Son.

From death to life by your spoken Word
    those who are scoffers may say it's absurd
But this simple child found the grace to believe.
    You my Messiah, have set my soul free.

Easter has come
    bringing dawn to my heart
chains of the past
    disappear — new life starts.

New joy has risen that knows no end.
    Praise you my savior . . . .
               my healer . . . .
                    my friend . . . .

Diane Thompson

Life's Adventure

It seems I am at a new plateau
I have walked far enough and can now look back and actually
      see the progress
What an encouragement!

Oh Lord,
the deeper the healing
the closer I am to knowing You more
to being wholly Yours
to knowing freedom.

At each plateau
      I notice the air is sweeter
            the vistas are greater and more majestic.

I never knew there were lands such as these I trod.

Life with You, Lord,
is an adventure
unfolding within myself.

Rita McIlwain

Sweet Lord of Love —

At some Secret Time of Mystery

(Unknown to me)

You have Blessed my Heart

With YOUR TOUCH;

And given me

In answer to my Deepest Plea

and undeserving Prayers —

Enclosed in tears and thorns

Brokenness — and sighs of no translation . . . . .

A PRICELESS GIFT! . . . . . A TENDER HEART.

Dorothy M. Owen

Another year has sped away!

I clean the chamber of my heart —

So White —

So Immaculate!

I shout my Resolutions

I paint them on the walls of my mind;

I sing them

With my feet resting on Carpeted Floor;

I Pray them;

I say, See Lord!   Hear Lord!

HE smiles

HE speaks —

"Take My Hand, Make no vow

Or empty Pledge that arises

In the Thick and Darkened Smoke of Empty Sound!

Take My Hand and we will walk —

One Small Step

One Small Step

Into the unformed Mystery

Of your next moment of Life!"

Dorothy M. Owen

Looking Forward — Looking Back

I couldn't laugh,
  I couldn't cry;
I couldn't live,
  I couldn't die.
I felt all wrong,
  mistake each way,
I never knew
  just what to say —
I needed some encouragement,
  I needed gentle care,
I needed somehow just to know,
  that someone else was there.
I grew and learned —
  to spread my wings,
To search for answers
  for puzzling things.
My quest, though painful,
  couldn't make me quit.
I looked and rummaged
  for pieces that fit.
The more I asked
  the more I knew.
The more it helped
  the more I grew.

Eve Bailey

Reflections

Who is this woman
that I see
locked in the mirror. . .
looking at me?

Bright streaks of silver
in her hair —
wrinkles and creases,
etched here and there.

The past years have flown
oh so fast,
it's only memories
that seem to last.

Grasp the successes —
seal the bad,
remember the smiles —
and face the sad.

I've learned something new —
healing this way,
the bright adventure —
that dawns a new day.

Eve Bailey

A Broken Heart Finds Peace

The pain I felt was so intense

I was so sad, so lonely

Till the Holy Spirit took control

Now He's the One and Only.

A broken heart I gave to Him,

with all insecurities and fears

He, in turn, restored to me

once more the flood of tears.

Oh the beauty of His presence

It's so precious and so dear

May I never lose the wonder

Of my Saviour year to year.

The Holy Spirit now controls

He lives within my soul

He gives me love, His joy, and peace

[continued]

For Heaven is my goal.

My feet now dance along the way

my body's now in tune

Oh praise His wondrous, gracious Name!

He's coming very soon!

Joan Maasbach

Intimacy: [With] Jesus

Because We're Friends

The truest friend I have today
I have as heaven's gift;
His name is Jesus Christ
who stays
Beside me lest I drift.

No man cares for me like Him —
I cry and no one hears;
But He has proved Himself my friend
By sharing all my tears.

For it is He alone who sees
Where the pain begins;
He speaks such gentle words to me
Because we are true friends.

Oh, Jesus, Friend, I only care
That all my heart you see;
For it is You who takes the time
To be a friend to me.

When I weep, my precious Lord,
I thank you that you hear,
While in my pain — you still remain
The only friend who's near!

Kenneth R. Thompson

Lord,

As I find delight in you,

As I praise your majesty, power, and strength,

As I trust every moment to you. . .

I am filled with awe and wonder,

I am able to find peace and joy,

I am humbled as the desires of my heart are fulfilled.

I am grateful

    thankful

    delighted

    overjoyed

And full of gratitude

    adoration

    praise

    and appreciation.

To you, be the glory. Amen.

(Adaption of Psalm 37:4)

Jackie Bush

A Love Song

It took a long time to hear it —
The notes of a love song fall flat on a heart of stone,
fail to penetrate deafened ears.

It would seem that a loveless soul
would soak up such grand overtures of love
like rain falling on parched ground.

Love is not to be trusted, however.
It must be frisked to reveal concealed weapons,
interrogated to determine its motives.

You continued to play the song,
and the melody found its way quietly,
gently into the chambers of my well-guarded heart.

You played on as the warmth of each note
began to melt the thick walls of ice,
and soothed my raging fears.

Timidly, and almost without realizing
I heard my own voice begin to harmonize
with that tender, irresistible melody.

The strains were tentative and somewhat off-key,
but as the ice melted and trickled away
the refrain swelled into full chorus.

At times the notes still seem strange,
my voice wavering in fear
as past images dance before my eyes.

But for the heart that has tasted Divine Love,
there can be no returning to the fortress of fear and
isolation . . .
            that once, was its home.

Judy Johnson

When yet life was young

And pink bubble gum

And Teddys and Clowns

Brought me Joy;

I was tutored by sages

On "how to make wages"

On "how to succeed"

Just where to "weed"

Just how to "impress"

To "step over the Mess,"

To gain much acclaim;

To set forth MY NAME!

But, let me explain —

One day I just chose

To walk through a field;

(I think I just chose,

Or did I yet yield?)

Was it planned that I respond

[continued]

To a Voice quite close by?

Beckoning Hand, Wind's Breath, a Deep sigh?

What matter — I found something there in that place,

That nothing of worldliness can ere deface,

Now naught else can ever — will ever suffice,

MY JESUS HAD SHOWN ME HIS PEARL OF GREAT PRICE!

Dorothy M. Owen

Just Because Of Who You Are

Please stop bringing Me
    the striving gifts.
The gifts you work on
    long and hard,
That knot your stomach,
    and tax your brain.
The gifts upon which
    you think hang
    the price tag of your worth.

Bring me instead
    your still gifts.
Your quiet time of rest,
Your walks of awe
    through My treasure-laden world.
Your heartbeats of joy,
    as the light goes on
    in someone's eyes,
    simply for seeing you.

That alone should tell you
    what I long for!
Not time consuming successes —
Not top of the heap accomplishments —
Just the light going on in your soul
    as you greet Me
    for who l am,
And the longing in your heart
    to spend time with Me
Just because of who you are.

Betty Reber

Gifts

Gifts!

Gifts!

Look at the gifts

Under the Christmas tree!

Gifts!

Gifts!

Marvelous gifts,

Can I open mine up and see?

Wonder glorious wonders,

How did this come to be . . . .

Because of His life,

Because of His death,

Because He has risen in me!

Kay Kocour

High Places Of His Grace

High and lifted up

your goodness touches me

bathes my eyes in tears of joy

inlays my heart with loveliness

etched, a mind of purity

fills my soul with holiness.

High and lifted up

your grace to me abounds

fills my life with fruitful days

fills my mouth with songs of praise

melody, harmony then symphony

of heavenly praise.

Within your sanctuary

your Spirit comforts me

comes to me quietly

tenderly cleanses me

faithfully looses me

and joyfully sets me free.

Kay Kocour

Sunday Morning Service

I felt the Spirit of God move in church that day,
the touch of Jesus.

I saw faces reflecting that touch as mirrors reflect an image —
And in that image I saw tears, cleansing tears,
washing away the pain, as a spring rain washes away the muck.

And in the images of others, I saw glory —
a wonderful light, a glowing, glorious light,
shining from within the depths of the soul.

And somewhere amidst the glory and the tears,
amidst the splendor and the shame —
I saw the Fingerprints of Jesus —
The Touch of God that exists under the pleasure,
under the pain, under the laughter,
and under the tears.

The Touch of God that cannot be erased by the hands of disaster,
nor the imprint of success.

And I know that God is real.
God is real in the midst of pain,
God is real in the midst of sorrow,
And God is real in the midst of Glory.

And somewhere amidst the Glory and the tears,
I heard the Voice of Jesus.

"For our God is a consuming fire." (*Hebrews 12:29*, KJV)

Rita Lee

Thank You

How can I say thank you, Dear LORD,
For the way You have blessed me?
What can I say, do, think or pray
That can even begin to repay You?
You have given to me freely and with
No strings attached . . .
I do not deserve such loving attention
But Your grace and mercy reveal Your love.
Every blessing, every treasure is
Laid up for me because You are
In me and I in You.
I am prone to wander, yet You keep
Calling me, and always make me
Feel so welcome when I return to You.
How can You do that when You
See the way I am?
Forgive me when I look at things
From my earthly perspective . . .
I want to see things from Your view, and
In order to do that I must stay
Close to You.
Help me to ask, to seek, to obey and to
Know more and more of You, as we walk
Earth's paths together.
I long to accept all that happens with joy
Because of You, Dear Father.
It is possible, as I trust in You.
Perhaps that is how I can thank You.
Help me fix my eyes on You.

Jo Winkowitsch

Intimacy: [With] Others

By their fruits

   you shall know them

By their roots

   you shall understand them.

Betty Reber

Ode To A Gentle Spirit

I always thought

I'd taken a stone

tied it to your memory

and tossed it into the sea.

I now realize

the sea exists today

because of all the tears

I've shed in your honor.

Should we chance to meet again

when the Lord takes me home

as He took you so many many years ago,

I'll tell you what your smile means to me

by pointing to the sea.

Kay Kocour

The Secret Of Love

Let's climb the highest mountain
        And reach up for the peak,
Looking to our Jesus,
        Whose presence we all seek.

There are just two clear pathways.
        So, which way should we go?
One is smooth and easy,
        The other, rough, I know.

He sent us up the rough one,
        To make us brave and strong,
But He was always with us;
        We knew that all along.

He longed to show His children,
        The secret of His love.
He knew that we would find it
        Among the peaks above.

After the long hard journey
        We finally reached the top.
It's here we found the secret —
        His Words carved on a rock.

So, if we want to please Him,
        This one thing we must do.
Just live the words He etched there —
        "Love others, as I've you."

Joanne Warren

Words To Heal

Lord, give me words to heal
    the wounded, and bandages
of hope to cover their scars.

Give me, Lord, a torch of inspiration
    to usher someone through
the dark tunnel of despair,
    hands that heal the scars
and dissipate their fears . . .

Eyes to see beyond the mask
    the painted smiles they wear . . .
Eyes to pierce the veil of pain
    and a prayer cloth for their tears.

Give me an ointment of love, a balm
    to mend the broken hearts,
a candle of courage to light the path
    when the night is dark.

Give me fortitude to fight
    a flame of doubt
with a flame of faith . . .
    courage to tell the world
of Your amazing grace.

Give me wisdom to differentiate
    between a dream and reality
Discernment to know whatever comes
    in my life You've allowed to be.

Give me strength to run this race
    though the finish line be far
for I long to be all that You've made me
    and become everything You are.

Gladys Washington

Inasmuch

The Lord is coming to live at our house.
He is old and tired and frightened.
He is 79 and alone.
He hurts a lot
and gets sick easily.
He gets frustrated over
       loss of energy
          and loss of memory,
a bending back,
being away from His home
       of 60 years,
the loss of personal things,
His departing friends,
dependency on others
       even to ride
       or having His hair washed.
So He is coming to live with us.
We have opportunity to serve Him,
       love Him, comfort Him, and
       care for Him.
He may live here many years,
       or just a few,
But we must never forget
       who He is.
He is Jesus,
       clothed in my mother,
And bringing to us
       a moment by moment reminder

    of INASMUCH.

    ". . . Inasmuch as ye have done it unto
      one of the least of these my brethren,
  ye have done it unto me." (*Matthew 25:40*, KJV)

Betty Reber

Intimacy: [With] Ourselves

Betty May

Betty May
    don't make me stay away.
    These are our
        come together days!
    Light the closet
    Remove the door
    Empty the boxes
    On the floor.
    Be rid of what
    We need no more.
    Now we'll gather
    Things all new
    Coming from both
    me and you.
    Now, we're one
    no longer two.

Betty Reber

Contrasts

May the small portion
of the picture of time
on which I gaze
at this brief moment,
be but a reminder to me
of the great artistry
that paints the whole spectrum
of the masterful design.

May the dark colors
of today
blend into the whole picture,
to make it
that much more
complete and glorious.
How dull, a painting done
all in golds and yellows.
But how lovely they are
splashed across
the black and purple contrasts.

Oh, let me not dictate
how the artist
blends the colors,
but enjoy to the fullest
each brush stroke.
Knowing confidently
that the whole intricate plan
will be breathtakingly
beautiful.

Betty Reber

Friends At Last!

The little girl within becomes frantic
Sometimes, and cries for someone to
Understand her when no words can be spoken.
And I have finally admitted she's me.
Trauma has blocked out for years
The part of me that remembers . . .
Yet I see the past stealing in to affect
Attitudes, reactions and countless ideas.
Now I work to let these memories exist
So I can envision and deal with her feelings.
For I am finally willing to remember —
To allow whatever emotions that may appear
In our meeting and living together . . .
For they would be better than this
Hard numbness that often bothers.
The child in me must grow up so I can
Become the woman God wants me to be.
But I do struggle to recognize this girl . . .
To understand her . . . encourage her . . .
Calm her . . . without anger or guilt.
— For all she's ever wanted was to be
Freely accepted and loved.
I have been avoiding her for years,
Hoping she would go away, even
Trying to kill her in my effort to live.
But now I see I will only become free
As she is released from her prison.
I am committed to becoming someone
She can talk to and trust . . .
For she has been waiting alone too long
It is time for us to become friends . . .
Friends at last.

Jo Winkowitsch

Peace

Sliver Of Dawn

A sliver of dawn — a sliver of dawn,
no, no — no more, that's all I can take —
a sliver of dawn, a sliver of dawn.
Exposed I flee the night of morn, the light of morn.

It's time, my child, I take that sliver of dawn
add the blue blue from the sky and fill those deep dark empty
eyes.
Skin of bronze kissed by the sun, I'll wrap in arms of
compassion's love —
hear now the psalms within the trees, captured on a distant
breeze,
see them float on bended knees and find a home at last.

Add the dreams on a thousand stars
infused in the incarnate word — forge a sword of steel!
Strengthen loin, leg and chest with courage that endures the test,
reach out now in confidence — touch a heart for me.

Frailty, fears, a fragile mind
no longer shattered — scattered in rhyme
restored yet shadowed until the time of my everlasting glory.

DOUSED — the flames of Hinnom's shame!
Drink now from The Dragon's Well — the serpent's underfoot.

REJOICE!

Your past has passed.

Kay Kocour

I Am Loved

I praise You Heavenly Father
You **are** good.
You **are** pure and loving.

You **are** in the sun that is at this very moment shining in the
      cold March sky
      giving hope of spring that is sure to come.
You **are** a God of hope.

You **are** in the conversation of the birds I now hear
      even the fat-bellied robins who have piloted themselves
      into my yard today — offering a fresh new season of life.
You **are** a God of life and new seasons.
You **are** God.
You **are** my God.

I curl up on Your lap and breathe in the security of peace
      and beauty and safety.

I am free.

I am loved.

Rita McIlwain

The Funeral Of Sparrows

My Father cares for sparrows,
Their funerals He attends.
For He is always present,
When their life journey ends.

Why did He tell the secret,
Of care for little birds?
So He could share with humans,
His love in simple words.

Our hairs they all are numbered,
Our steps are measured too.
So we can know the blessings,
Of trusting mercies too.

Our breaths, He watches o'er them,
Each heart beat He does see;
We're made in His own image,
Bound for eternity.

If birds sing for their Maker,
Should we not raise a song?
To glorify our Father,
And praise Him all day long?

(Reverend Kendal was a Hebrew Christian who wrote this poem
while on a dialysis machine in his early seventies. He has now
recovered from his tremendous pain, for he is with his Messiah.)

Rev. Fred Kendal

Peace In My Soul

Special peace . . . untouched, softening the heart,

gradually filling one's soul,

as a river making its way downstream;

Smooth . . . graceful . . . inviting, no disturbances —

pleasing in every movement;

Beauty abounding, a touch of radiance . . .

reflecting His beauty and creative calm;

Flowing waters, cool, fresh breeze,

guiding individual waves over polished rocks.

A river's life: Of trust and beauty.

Needs supplied, triumphant living . . .

Peace, His Peace, as a river in my soul.

Julie Civitts

Heaven

Ultimate Heaven

How passed is past?
When at will,
    we can visit and wander,
    — it lives.
No moment is gone
    that is stored in memory.
No moment is wasted . . .
    that energizes the present.
Perhaps heaven is
    that endless period
    when we can relive
    any moment in time,
And choose the way
    —we wish it had been.
The ultimate heaven, then,
    —we wouldn't choose
    to change it.

Betty Reber

The Promise

I spent the night in heaven
I know, I saw you there
coming to me o'er jeweled paths
through fields of flowers fair
and hand in hand we deftly steal
into the storehouses of the snow
sculpting, launching,
sliding, skating, laughing
our cheeks aglow
with mutual affection,
love denied so young
yet still alive and waiting
My Lord Jesus come and
make this dream a reality
give this promise actuality . . . .

all too soon the dawn, she beckons my return
and through a window of time climb I
yonder many years
and awake I upon a pillow
no longer soaked with tears.

Kay Kocour

Rending The Veil

I have a problem . . . it's with my grip. I hold on too tightly and far
    too long . . .
long after signs of life are gone — long into the night
— long into the next day . . .
days pass, years, I'm still holding on . . .
long since ligament, tendon and bone have ceased to function.

It's been so long I've forgotten what it is I hold.
As I try to look, my hand is fixed — frozen into a fist —
(fingers paralyzed around, fingernails ingrown into the flesh,
knuckles flexed and taut). There is no feeling left . . .
my hand has turned to stone!

It was you who touched me . . . asked if you could see what was in
    my hand.
I wasn't sure at first, but as the warmth of your smile penetrated
    my heart,
I thought I'd take a chance.
My arm moved with the grace of a tin soldier and I was scared too,
for I distinctly remember . . . whatever it was felt dark and slimy
and from within voices chided and warned against exposure.
"Are you sure you want to see?" I asked. "I don't think it's pretty."

I even remember letting someone peek inside once. Her fearless
    courage soon withered.
"I never promised you anything," she said. Perhaps I expected too
    much.

Through the years, through the tears still you stayed, and the
    longer you stayed,
the more fleshlike my hand became . . . pinkish tan in color and
bluish veins!!
Could that be a sign that the blood of life had at last
returned into my hand??

Then one day it happened.
From within I felt it stir. Panic was my first response!
You were there as always . . . calming me.
But in a fit of independence I flung my arm skyward,
watching in awesome wonder as my hand began to open —
and a winglike creature glistening of red, blue and yellow shades
emerged, escaped, and rending the veil between earth and sky . . .
disappeared into the light!

"What was that?" I asked. "Whatever it is, it's free now," you
    answered.
"Do you suppose that was me?" "Why don't you follow me and
    see," you said.
As I turned to see where you were going, you too
    looked skyward . . .
and rending the veil between earth and sky, disappeared into the
    light!

I lunged, and able now with opened hand
grasped the hem of your garment and like a laser's flash,
rent the veil between earth and sky . . . and disappeared into the
    light!

Kay Kocour

The Year Of The Lord's Favor

1991 . . . . Who would have ever guessed the promise in Joel that drew me to Jesus Christ in 1972 would be so abundantly fulfilled? Not a gift here and there as before but a showering of blessings over me like bright light and sparkling joy.

"I will restore to you the years the locust have eaten in your life and you will not be ashamed."

Yes, He has and is and will be forever. Amen.

My greatest blessing is the love I have with Jim. He is in my heart and soul and spirit and a growing blessing every day. Thank You, Jesus.

My precious sons are being released now to live their lives without me holding on. I'm entrusting them to You, Lord and I can rest and enjoy my life more, too. Thank You for this grace.

I value myself deeply and continue to get to know myself in healthy relationships and in times alone. I like the person You made me to be. Thank You, Jesus.

The lost relationships have been returned to me in new ones, multiplied, blessed and overflowing. Why did I doubt and hold on so long? Thank You, Lord Jesus, for Your grace in my doubt.

Favor and tangible rewards have come to me early where I work. You have brought me love and respect, especially by men. How I have needed healing in that area. You are a very wise and protective Good Shepherd. Thank You, again.

I can accept my parents and have good boundaries of love with them now. Your grace is abundant.

To hear and trust my heart where Jesus speaks is a fulfilled desire as I can also hear Your words at times for others that they might be blessed. Praise be to God.

Scripture stored in my mind and heart during the years of pain are there to bless me, as well as those You bring into my life. I thank You, Lord.

The world's ways tug at me but I can say, "No," I'm choosing Christ's Way. For this strength, I thank You.

The boldness, at last, to proclaim Jesus, take His rebuff from others and praise Him openly is taking hold. Glory to You, Lord Christ!

My need to caretake other people is being healed. I did it to feel valuable. I am valuable because I am Yours — You died for me. You created me.

Faith in God's goodness to me now and forever is sure. My doubts lessen. The steps I will take on earth, I can trust You to show me and trust myself to hear.

And so, for all these things, and especially for love, I lift my heart and my hands in thanksgiving for all You are, have been, and will be, unto me. Amen.

Diane Thompson

POETRY INDEX

Support

Perseverance

Endurance

two PROVISIONS

Hope

Faith

three THE JOURNEY

Denial / Shock

Anger

Betrayal

Shame / Doubt

Guilt

Loss / Sadness

Acceptance

Forgiveness

four OBSTACLES

Discouragement

Pride

Compromise

Aimlessness

Ridicule

Rejection

Unbelief

Impatience

Hopelessness

five REWARDS

Purpose

Renewed Vitality

Intimacy:

[With] Jesus

[With] Others

[With] Ourselves